The Subject Was Roses

About Those Roses or *How* Not *To Do a Play and Succeed*

and the text of *THE SUBJECT WAS ROSES*

FRANK D. GILROY

Random House   *New York*

BOOKS BY FRANK D. GILROY

Who'll Save the Plowboy?
The Subject Was Roses

FOR
My Mother
AND
My Father

About Those Roses
or
How *Not* To Do a Play and Succeed

Prologue

The Subject Was Roses was written in Hollywood (between screen jobs) in the winter of 1960 and the spring, summer and fall of 1961. It was polished in the winter of 1961–62 and sent to my New York agent (Blanche Gaines) on April 19, 1962.

During April, May and June it was submitted to several well-known producers and returned with no expression of interest. These producers now, without exception, say they never read or even heard of the play. In each instance, investigation bears them out: it was a reader, or someone at a similar echelon, who passed judgment in the producer's name.

On July 1, 1962, the play was optioned by Leonard Soloway and Richard Altman for production on Broadway. The Phoenix Theatre, which produced my first play, Who'll Save the Plowboy?, was to participate. Dan Petrie, who directed Plowboy, was engaged as director. Keir Dullea expressed a strong desire to play the son's role. All we needed was an actor to play the father, and an actress to play the mother.

On October 16, 1962, we were still looking for a father and mother.

On October 17, 1962, I commenced a daily journal. The entries concerning Roses were incidental.

3

PROLOGUE

On May 25, 1964, *The Subject Was Roses* opened on Broadway with a producer who had never produced a Broadway play; a director who had never directed one; a scenic artist who had never designed one; a general manager who had never managed one; and three actors who were virtually unknown.

In the weeks since, I've extracted the material about *Roses* from my journal; deleted what was mean, libelous or offensive; and now append the remainder for those who like fairy tales.

October 17, 1962

One more note—on *Roses* still no casting progress. We have been turned down by Malden, E. G. Marshall, Matthau, Kennedy, Dan Dailey, Maureen Stapleton, Judy Holliday, Geraldine Page, Teresa Wright, and Lord knows who else. Trying Edmond O'Brien and Van Heflin. After that?

October 19

Roses went to O'Brien yesterday.

October 26

No word on *Roses* this week.

October 28

Leonard met Art Carney last night about *Roses*. I wonder what happened? *Roses* gone to Eileen Heckart.

October 31

Leonard called yesterday, no word from anyone. Wants to go after ———. He spoke to Dan Petrie, who is in England. Dan most reluctant about ———. It would be a big gamble but if we could make that old shoe dance—what a triumph! Dan suggested I meet ——— and evaluate him in person. He also granted Leonard and Dick a ten-day extension on date when they must tell him whether we go or not. Now that we approach a deadline of sorts, things begin to happen—and that is the pattern preceding the best

5

things that have happened to me. Me, a magical thinker? Now, doctor.

(Later)

Heckart turned the play down. Carney turned it down.

November 1, 1962

Dick called last evening—suggested two actresses I'd vetoed earlier. I vetoed them again. A week from tomorrow the boys (Dick and Leonard) must have something nailed down or the whole project collapses. And that perhaps for the best?

November 2

No word on *Roses* yesterday.

November 3

Oh yes—Ruth Gordon's name came up yesterday, via Blanche. They'll investigate, although I don't remember what she looks like.

November 4

This next week tells the story on a *Roses* production for this year. Why am I sanguine? Am I hoping to junk the producers and Dan? If so, for what? Or do I just enjoy prolonging the whole production process so that I always have something to look forward to—and can, at the same time, moan the injustice of it all?

November 5

This is the crucial week. Have a hunch ——— could be our man.

November 6

No call from Leonard yesterday about ———. Only four more shopping days left till Dan's "Note" falls due.

November 7

Leonard called. Lunch with ——— tomorrow. Lucy Kroll (Dan Petrie's agent) has some "important" word from

Dan which she wants to communicate to Leonard, Dick and me face-to-face.

November 9

The meeting with Lucy Kroll started unpromisingly. She catalogued all the old terrain, then got to the point: Dan highly opposed to ——, suggests Eddie Albert, Trevor Howard and Dan Duryea. I can't see Albert in the part. I like Howard, but Dick, Leonard and T. Edward thought he was too English. I bowed to that. Then to Duryea. I found this an excellent thought. Leonard had mentioned him months ago, and I was agreeable but we were pursuing "bigger fish" at the time and Duryea was forgotten. I said I would now offer the part to him without interview or reservation. Dick agreed. Lucy, who represents him, called Duryea in California—told him the script was coming. "This is the play I would like to bring you back to New York in," she said. Duryea said he'd call her Sunday. If he says no, then we are quite up the creek. All came from the interview with a surge of expectation. Lunch with ——.

Stopped at Blanche's—filled her in. Then to Leonard's office and a call to Dan Petrie, in London. Told Dan the entire day's events. "Yes," he would accept Duryea, but with "a question mark" that made me suspect that the idea of Duryea (rather than originating with him, as Lucy presented it) came from her.

November 10

Tomorrow is D-Day. How can Duryea say no?

November 11

D-Day. But for some reason I feel the matter will not be decided today. Leonard called at 2:00 P.M. to say that Duryea had read the play three times, liked it, but couldn't see himself in all parts of it. According to Leonard, Lucy is angry with Duryea, attacked the "Hollywood people" and their standards, feels she can talk him into it, but doesn't want to. I give her credit for that. Duryea is not out entirely: a mutual friend of his and Lucy's (knowledgeable) is to read the script tomorrow—then advise him.

November 12

Went to bed feeling vaguely ill. A large part of this probably due to the Duryea reaction. Thought it didn't matter that much.

November 13

Realize how lousy I felt yesterday, by how good I feel today. Leonard called: No word from Lucy beyond Sunday's. Would I meet Robert Preston just to talk if he read the script and were interested. Yes, if they insist.

November 15

No word yesterday. What the devil's happening?

November 16

Called Leonard at four o'clock yesterday. Duryea sent the script back. A script has gone to Albert and to Preston. I said I would meet them if they were interested, but warned Leonard again that I feel they are both wrong, and that if a meeting didn't alter these feelings, I would not be, could not be, pressured into accepting them.

November 18

Nothing on *Roses*.

November 20

No word on *Roses*. Meaning?

November 21

Dan should be back from England soon.

November 22 (Thanksgiving Day)

Then home and word from Leonard that Eddie Albert didn't like the play but that Preston likes it very much; was quite lavish in praise. Very flattering, but I must summon the courage to veto him if a meeting doesn't give me a ray of the character I wrote. Perhaps I will not have to make any decision since Preston is going to talk it over with his agent on Monday. Should the agent want him to do it, then I'm in for a great bombardment on all sides. If I can see that ray, I will say OK, but will I have the guts to say no? We'll see. In any case, it's encouraging to know a good actor likes it. According to Leonard, Preston said "it was the best thing offered to him this year" (is that a compliment?) and he felt it was bound to be a success, no matter who acted it. That is, he felt it didn't need names. Dan gets back a week from tomorrow.

November 24

Blanche called. Already the pressure about Preston.

November 25

Suspect strongly that I will accept Preston if the opportunity is offered.

November 26

A nice visit here with Blanche, Leonard and Dick yesterday. They wisely refrained from all but the most casual reference to Preston.

November 27

Dick called—Preston is seeing his agent Wednesday night.

November 29

Preston met with his agent to discuss *Roses* last night. I feel he will not do it. This would both relieve and disappoint.

November 30

Leonard called yesterday. Preston said no. Due, according to Leonard, to the age of the character. Preston appended the usual "He's the most talented writer around. Please let me see his next play," etc., etc., etc. I did not expect to feel so relieved by his refusal as I do. Is it because

9

his refusal prolongs the whole experience? It's fun and safe to be so potential. Leonard and Dick were understandably depressed; suggested a lot of actors not right at all. Dan arrives today. We might all confer over the weekend. Took five years to get *Plowboy* on. I have as much confidence in *Roses*.

December 2, 1962

Leonard called. He'd spoken to Dan. We'll meet Tuesday at two. I called Dan to welcome him home. He sounded in good spirits.

December 5

Then to Leonard's office for the meeting. Dick and Leonard there. Dan arrived a half hour late. He'd stopped at the Gaiety Delicatessen—spotted Pat Hingle and joined him. Hingle wondered why he hadn't seen Dan around. Dan said he'd been in England doing pictures—had gone over there right after *Plowboy* opened. Hingle said, "I've just read another play by Gilroy." Dan did not inform him of his connection with that "new play." Asked Hingle how he happened to read it. Hingle said Bob Preston had given it to him for an opinion, as to whether he, Preston, should do it. Hingle's appraisal: he liked the script, but thought Broadway had priced itself out of the luxury of such plays. Therefore he advised Preston against doing it. Dan now felt obliged to reveal his link with the play. Hingle said, "Well, I bet I'll put my foot in it once more before sundown." About the meeting: We went over and over the list of actors to no avail. I turned to Dan, asked him to "give me that fine actor who isn't a name, who you've been saving for an emergency." He came back with Joe Anthony, the actor turned director, who is a close friend of his. We had tried to get Joe to direct *Roses* when it seemed Dan was not available. I was told then that he liked the play but didn't want to intrude on Dan's preserve.

December 6

Called Swanie to discuss *Beau Geste* deal with Universal. Told him an absolute prerequisite was time off to do *Roses*. He called last night—OK on time for *Roses*. Ruth paid bills and gave me a financial report which eliminates any thought of turning *Beau Geste* down and gambling all on *Roses*.

December 7

Dan called. Joe Anthony feels *Roses* needs a lot of work. I told Dan that since I saw no need for revisions until after the first reading, and that I expected they would be minimal, it was obvious we and Anthony were too far apart. I phoned Blanche to inform her of what happened; turned out Dan had called her earlier. They'd discussed Anthony's rejection, and pretty much decided between them that *Roses* belongs off-Broadway. Most melancholy about all this and my imminent departure for the Coast.

December 8

Dan met with Dick and Leonard yesterday; told them he thought a lot of things in *Roses* needed spelling out for uptown. The boys said they opposed any changes.

December 9

I leave for Los Angeles today. The Petries arrived here at noon yesterday. I told Dan that Leonard and I felt he had considerable reservations about the script and our plans in general. I said I wouldn't consider off-Broadway for several years. He said he'd think all this over and talk to Leonard and Dick in my absence. Leonard called last night—said Jason Robards had read the script and would "like to be associated with it." Robards is meeting or phoning Leonard Monday, at which time the extent and nature of his interest will be determined. Now to California.

December 11—Hollywood

Saw Keir Dullea. Spoke to him, we might lunch today.

Leonard called. He saw Robards, who is considering *Roses* for next fall. Wants to meet me first.

December 15—Hollywood

Ruth called. Said that Leonard informed her that Quintero would like to direct the play with Robards.

December 21—Hollywood

Beau Geste treatment finished. Flying home tonight. Meeting Robards at 11:00 A.M. Monday.

December 24—Home

I'm on a bus en route to New York to meet Robards at Leonard's office. I had a frank talk with Dan yesterday: told him we were exploring the possibility of Robards and Quintero.

December 25 (Christmas)

Robards failed to show up yesterday. At eleven-twenty we received a call from Lauren Bacall saying simply that he couldn't be there.

December 26

Leonard called last night. We are meeting Robards at Dinty Moore's on Friday at 1:00 P.M.

December 29

Leonard and Dick at Moore's when I arrived. A call from Lauren Bacall, to inform us that Jason would be twenty minutes late. He arrived a half hour late. Wore a white shirt with red stripes which he had gotten as a Christmas present and was self-conscious about. We assured him it was becoming. Early in the meeting, when we were all fidgeting with our knives and forks, I tried to cut to the heart of the thing: told Jason there was no actor I admired more than himself—that if he wanted the part it was his. He said he was considering several projects and was in no position to commit himself immediately. We assured him, falsely, that we hoped for no decision on the spot. Leonard told him that Quintero seemed anxious to do the play. Robards' interest was stimulated by this. He said he would get in touch with José after *Desire* opened. Later, when he realized I was leaving town on the 6th, he said he might intrude on Quintero's rehearsal time and get us together before I went.

December 31

Dick called yesterday morning to say that Quintero could see me for a drink at five-thirty last night. Beyond that he had no available time. I told Dick I couldn't make it—told him I was free any other day this week at José's convenience. Robards and Quintero know that we want them, and know that I'm leaving town next Sunday. The next move is theirs.

January 1, 1963

Dick called yesterday to say we had a date at Quintero's home at noon today if I could make it. I said yes.

January 2

Met Quintero, liked him. Impressed by his candor: "I have no commitments next fall. I want to do this play with or without Jason." There was a good air about our conversation—a nice way to launch the new year. Dick was as pleased by the meeting as I was.

January 6

Nice talk with Dan on phone. Brought him up to date. To Hollywood tomorrow.

January 13—Hollywood

No word on *Roses*.

January 18—Hollywood

Then to UCLA to see *Burlesque* with Jack Albertson. It was sheer delight, largely due to Jack's performance. He communicated a character which far surpassed the material. Went backstage to tell Jack how much I enjoyed his work. Also I wanted a close look at him, because I suspect he could be right for *Roses*.

January 23—Hollywood

Robards holding up decision on *Roses* until he reads Arthur Miller's new play, which has been offered to him.

January 25—Hollywood

Called Ruth. Lovely talk, lovely girl. She hears Robards likes Miller's play, but doesn't know if he can afford to do it at Lincoln Center.

January 30—Hollywood

I called Ruth. Robards has given no word, but Dick and Leonard are most pessimistic. According to Blanche, they are suicidal.

February 8, 1963—Hollywood

Call from Leonard yesterday. He and Dick are "unable to eat or sleep." Robards still won't say yes or no. One of Leonard's backers is willing to put up all the money for a production this spring with ———. I vetoed it diplomatically. Told Leonard that I felt he was being stampeded into production. I reaffirmed my confidence in him and Dick and my willingness to wait. We decided on two steps: first, try to sign Quintero and Keir Dullea for next fall. If that doesn't work, then we'll explore English production possibilities. Leonard sounded much cheered by all this.

February 14—Hollywood

Blanche called. David Selznick wants to read *Roses* as a possibility for his wife, Jennifer Jones.

February 16—Hollywood

Letter from Dick Altman, saying that Quintero wouldn't sign until casting was set. He said Colleen Dewhurst likes it, but doesn't want to do it.

March 26, 1963—Home

Supposed to meet Quintero about *Roses* some night this week.

March 31

Dick Altman called last night. We will meet Quintero tomorrow night at six-fifteen at his apartment.

April 2, 1963

Leonard called to inform that Quintero had canceled our meeting. Went to Leonard's office: learned that Jason had turned us down—sent the script back. Edmond O'Brien sent the script back after five months without reading it. Had supper with George Morrison at the Limelight. Bill Snyder joined us. Both felt my producers were remiss in not trying to cajole and pressure desired actors like Jason into doing *Roses*. I feel it's demeaning to have to sell it in that way. Am I being a fool?

April 4

I mentioned Jack Albertson to Dan Petrie. Dan knows Jack and responded most favorably.

April 10

David Wayne feels *Roses* is too depressing to play night after night. At least it was so reported by his agent. Quintero is still, according to his agent, eager to do the play. He will contact Robards personally upon Jason's return from his father's funeral. All of this comes to me through the boys.

April 18

Sent a copy of *Roses* to Jack Albertson via his nephew George Englund. I have a big hunch about Albertson.

April 20

Bill Liebling called Blanche—said Pat Hingle, having heard *Roses* was considerably rewritten, wanted to read it again. Blanche informed him that not a word was changed.

April 30

Jack Albertson wants to do the play. The only catch is an outside possibility that his TV series might be renewed. I called Dick. He was pleased by the news: told me he and Leonard had discussed Jack at length and were ready to accept him without a face-to-face interview.

May 1, 1963

Leonard phoned Albertson. Liked him. If the TV series is off, we're in business. I called Dan Petrie at the boys' suggestion. Yes, he would like to do the play on Broadway with Albertson.

May 7—Hollywood

Spoke at length to Albertson. He's raring to go, if he can get a release from Four Star on his TV series.

May 8—Hollywood

Lunched with Jack. He's pressing to get a written release from Four Star.

May 10—Hollywood

There is a clause in the Actors' Guild contract to the following effect: If Jack goes to Four Star with a bona-fide offer from another source, they must release him or put him on salary. He now has the offer (a telegram from Leonard and Dick) and is presenting it today.

May 15—Hollywood

Jack Albertson just called and said he'd spoken to Leonard Soloway, who offered him $750 a week. Jack specified no sum, but said that wasn't enough. The Phoenix Theatre has pulled out of the picture because Jack is no name.

May 18—Hollywood

Jack called yesterday morning. He hadn't heard from the boys, and was a bit fearful, I suspect, about jeopardizing the deal, with his salary demand. I assured him I was confident that it would all work out.

May 22—Hollywood

What a jolt! Leonard and Dick just called to say that Keir Dullea is not available, and that without his name none of their backers will spring for Jack. What I want them to do is sign Jack, and work from there—in short, I'm asking them to throw themselves off the building, which is the only way anything valid gets accomplished. They'll call me at 9:00 A.M. my time tomorrow to say yes or no.

May 23—Hollywood

The boys will not sign Jack and gamble on raising the rest of the money. I asked them to release the play. They did so. Two P.M.—Called Peter Nelson. Told him the situation, since he loves *Roses* and has always wanted to do it. His partner is picking up a script today. A call to Jack Albertson. What embarrassment to explain all this to him.

May 24—Hollywood

Dan Petrie called last night. The boys had notified him —he wanted my version. I gave it—sounding to myself like the Ancient Mariner. He could sympathize with their concern about taking the plunge. I suspect he might have been calling to sound me out on the possibility of letting the Phoenix do it. I indicated early in our talk that my sights were still on Broadway. I called Jack, related the whole thing to him. He could also sympathize with the boys' fear of gambling on *his* name. He was philosophical about his disappointment. I again told him how perfect I thought he was for the role and said I expected to see him play it one day. NOTHING HAPPENS EXCEPT THAT ONE MAN PURSUES A VISION FANATICALLY.

May 25—Hollywood

A most melancholy day yesterday. The reaction to all attending that rupture with the boys. Jack just called to say that Leonard called him—for which I'm glad. Leonard explained the whole thing; his only criticism of me is that I won't give him another year—or till next spring, which is the same thing. Marty Donovan is contacting Ely Landau about *Roses*. No word from Peter Nelson.

May 27—Hollywood

George Englund called—asked me what was happening with *Roses*. I told him. He sounded quite interested. Spoke of raising money, etc. We'll talk of that today. Special delivery letter from Blanche: a repeat of the boys' position—a hint that I am being unreasonable, etc.

May 28—Hollywood

Englund's plans for the play were to do it at Palm Beach —and some vague hint about money from Universal. I rejected both. Marty sent Landau a script and a case history to date. Peter Nelson objects a bit to Albertson—went away to reflect some more. A note from the boys this morning, along with the release, saying they wanted me to call when I got back to New York.

May 29—Hollywood

Called Ruth yesterday. She said Blanche wants to know how I feel about the boys continuing their efforts to get *Roses* on with Jack. I said fine, but I'll give them no exclusive.

May 30—Hollywood

Picked up *Roses* from Peter.

June 1, 1963—Hollywood

Getting a plane home today. Called Jack Albertson yesterday—planted possibility of off-Broadway in his mind if all else fails.

June 4—Home

Dan Petrie called—asked my feelings about having *Roses* done at the Phoenix. I said not at this time. Spoke to Ulu. He is sending *Roses* to a possible producer. If that man says yes, I will then have to make a decision, since part of that deal is that Ulu will direct.

June 5

I am seeing Leonard at noon. Meeting Ulu at six-thirty to give him *Roses*.

June 6

Went to Leonard's office yesterday. Dick there. A pleasant, amicable chat. All agreed that a breakdown of communication was the cause for the abrupt rupture—they should have kept me up to date on the developments about Keir and let me know how much they were banking on him. They feel they made the right decision—are still pursuing a production—but I think we all know that their moment with this play has passed.

June 7

Call from Dan Petrie. He called Maureen Stapleton, who is quite receptive to rereading *Roses*. She felt the mother's role was least significant of the three. Ulu called. The producer he has in mind arrives from England next Wednesday. Ulu realizes I'm exploring other avenues.

June 19

Ulu called to say the producer he had in mind said no, and was it all right to show it to Judy Rutherford? Sure.

June 27

Ulu told me yesterday morning that Judy Rutherford liked *Roses* but did not feel she could swing it at this time. Blanche called last night to say Judy's lawyer had called to inquire about the availability of *Roses*. What does that mean? Dan Petrie and I chatted. No word from Maureen Stapleton. The play circulates like a roulette ball—where will it come to rest?

July 2, 1963

Blanche called to say Judy Rutherford had called her

and is definitely interested in *Roses* for Broadway. She'll be calling me to talk of it and set up a meeting to talk further. She had told Ulu she didn't feel ready for Broadway, but her lawyer convinced her she was.

July 3

T. Edward Hambleton called to ask if I'd let them (he and Dan) do *Roses* at the Phoenix. I repeated what I'd said to Dan: I did not feel I had exhausted uptown possibilities.

July 7

Dick Altman called to say that he'd seen Patricia Neal in *Hud* and that she seemed fine for *Roses*.

July 8

Judy Rutherford called about *Roses*. Am meeting Ulu and her at Blanche's at two-thirty today. Saw *Hud* last night. Patricia Neal was superb. She certainly could play the mother in *Roses*.

July 9

Met Ulu and Judy at Blanche's yesterday. I told Judy I would not dispose of the play within the next three weeks, which will give her time to inventory her resources. At the end of that time, she must make a concrete offer or pass. Ulu is getting ready to (in his own words) "run with the play himself."

July 20

Just back from our trip to Nantucket. A letter from T. Edward asking me to have a talk with him about *Roses*.

July 23

Blanche called with some chat about *Roses*: Judy too involved to do it; Leonard still anxious to do it, etc. . . .

July 25

Ulu called. He's seeing lots of people about the play, but no luck so far.

August 3, 1963

Lunched with T. Hambleton yesterday. Told him I just didn't feel it was right to do *Roses* at the Phoenix now: if I said yes, I would be moving from weakness—from fear that otherwise it might not be done.

August 6

Blanche called. More pressure to do *Roses* off-Broadway.

August 18

Ulu called yesterday while I was out. Told Ruth he had someone interested in *Roses*. Would know by Tuesday.

August 19

Blanche says the boys are pursuing a money man—just as Ulu is.

September 7, 1963

Spoke to Blanche yesterday. Leonard and Dick think they can get the money with ——— in the mother's role. I said no. I feel that the producer of *Roses* has yet to appear.

September 13

Blanche called: Lars Schmidt wants to premier *Roses* in Sweden. It gives my ego a boost, but there is more to be lost than gained: if it's a flop, it will flag interest here—and I will never know *why* it flopped. The play as it stands is untested. I would surely alter it in production to arrive at a definitive version—which I can't do in Sweden. The thing I could gain: if a hit there, it would heighten interest here. But then I wouldn't know why it was a hit. Ruth concurs. Dick and Leonard sent a casting history on *Roses*. They list women their backers would support. Some of these women have already said no, but might be approached again: Page, Heckart, Stanley, Dewhurst. Another *Roses* note: John Crowther (Bosley's son) read it and liked it—would like to play the son's role. The ember glows.

September 19

Lunched with Ulu yesterday. He mentioned Carolyn Swan (who produced the Pinter plays), as being interested in his work. I suggested he mention *Roses* to her.

September 22

Saw Jack Albertson on TV (The Lieutenant) last night. It told nothing of his ability.

October 8, 1963

A fellow named David Black, who was reportedly interested in coproducing *Roses* (with Leonard), had a play (*Semi-detached*) open last night. If it succeeded he was going to back *Roses*. The radio capsule digest of reviews was thumbs down.

October 11

Leonard called to say Black was still interested in putting up money for *Roses*. He wanted to be sure that he and Dick still "had" the play. I said it was his till I told him differently—and surely through Monday, when he and Dick are meeting Black. He spoke of a January production. Ulu is to call soon. I want to let him know the play isn't available for the time being.

October 16

The boys met Black. Looks like he really wants in. I'm going to meet him tomorrow. I'm told he agrees to Albertson, but would like to see Dick Altman direct. That would leave Black and Leonard as sole producers. I got all this through Blanche. I anticipated the thing about Dick. His notices on the Betti play (*Corruption in the Palace of Justice*) were excellent.

October 18

Went up to Blanche's. Leonard arrived, followed by David Black. Black announced that the big toe on his left foot was purple—wondered if it might be due to the closing of *Semi-detached* this Saturday. I made it clear that Jack Albertson was a must—if he went along with that, then I would accept Dick as director. He agreed. We tried to call Jack, to see if he's available. He's on location at Big Bear with Elvis Presley. Leonard was going to call later when Jack's wife was home, to get the location number.

October 19

No word from Leonard about Jack Albertson. Suspect a new snag, and would guess that it concerns Black. Will call Leonard today.

October 20

Leonard contacted Jack. He's available, and will wire them as to which segment of Ensign O'Toole they should run for Black's inspection.

October 22

Jack never wired Leonard about the segment of O'Toole he wanted them to show Black. The boys did find one, and Black liked Jack. What does Jack's failure to telegraph mean? I am too suspicious. Blanche had a nice letter from Patricia Neal about *Roses* which she's forwarding.

October 23

Black *now* objects to Albertson's stature as a draw. I let him know my displeasure at this turnabout after alerting Jack. So here we are at the beginning again.

October 26

Called Blanche—asked her to get some statement of intention from Leonard about *Roses*.

October 27

Dick Altman called, told me they were waiting to hear from Haila Stoddard (Bonard Productions) about *Roses*. He says he and Leonard have twenty grand and a guy named Mel (or Max) has twenty more—but that both twenties are contingent on their getting another twenty.

October 31

Called Blanche. Dick is meeting Haila Stoddard about *Roses* (which she's read and liked) on Saturday. A copy of *Roses* came back from Carolyn Swan with a form note dated August and unsigned. Curious.

November 1, 1963

Leonard called to say that he'd called Jack Albertson and informed him things were progressing, but slowly. Jack was most understanding and passed his regards to me.

November 2

Dick called to chat before seeing Haila Stoddard today. I told him, in view of the Black thing, to make it *absolutely* clear that the play doesn't go without Jack.

November 3

Dick saw Haila Stoddard. She wants to be involved with the play, as a producer, whether her partner, Helen Bonfils, who is reading *Roses* this weekend, does or not. According to Dick, Haila knows Jack Albertson and thinks he's a good idea.

November 8

Dick Altman called. Haila Stoddard suggests a tryout of *Roses* in Arizona at the Sombrero Playhouse. I've considered such proposals before. I feel there is too much to be lost and nothing much gained. I sense that such an audience won't respond to this play, until it has an eastern stamp of approval. Boston and other tryout places here would be fine. But the West—no. Dick will be talking to her this afternoon, and will relay my thoughts.

November 10

Saw *Corruption in the Palace of Justice* last night— thought Dick's direction excellent.

November 19

I spoke to Dick. Leonard will get an associate producer

24

credit or one that reads "Bonard Productions in association with Leonard Soloway Presents." Bonfils is reportedly quite interested in acquiring rights for an independent movie production of *Roses*. Stoddard will now inform her of yesterday's talk with the boys. If there are no obstacles, it will be time for me to meet Stoddard, and talk contracts, etc. The boys are alerting Albertson once again. Could this finally be it?

November 21

Leonard called. We meet Stoddard at Sardi's at noon on Saturday. Some vague talk about ——, which I don't understand since they've already sent Jack Albertson a letter. If we go, it will be a February opening.

November 22

Spoke to Blanche and Leonard and Dick in separate calls yesterday morning. I was disturbed when I reflected on Leonard's mention of Stoddard's suggestion about ——. I wanted to make sure that I was not being invited to meet her tomorrow to talk about using someone other than Jack. The boys said Stoddard knew Jack, liked him, and thought he was a good idea. Now my antenna sensed a repetition of the Black experience. Leonard, when I called yesterday, felt Stoddard's mention of —— was just a passing thought. Blanche was not so reassuring. She informed me that she had met Stoddard on Tuesday, and that Stoddard said that Bonfils did not like *Roses* as much as she did. "Is this for off-Broadway?" was Bonfils' first thought. Told it wasn't, she apparently said she'd put up the money anyway. Then Blanche quoted Stoddard as saying she didn't know Jack Albertson or his work—had mistaken him for Frank Albertson. Blanche now repeated all the old arguments about my being unreasonable in my insistence on Jack, etc., etc. I told her that if this whole thing blew up over their acceptance of Jack now, it was

25

the final straw. I'm not sure what I mean by this. Well, in any case, I've let them know that I don't anticipate a discussion of Albertson's qualifications tomorrow.

November 23

The President was killed yesterday.

November 27

We met Stoddard as scheduled. She claimed to understand about Albertson (that he is a must) but I feel it will all come to nothing. It all seems so unimportant since Friday.

November 30

Call from Dick: Stoddard is having Gottlieb (their manager) read *Roses* over the weekend. Then what? Dick thinks all is going right. I feel nothing will come of it.

December 4, 1963

Called Blanche about *Roses*. She said I could expect a call from Stoddard. Gottlieb liked the play, but says we must have a female star to buttress Jack. The name to be presented was ———. Stoddard called. I vetoed ———. Said I had no objection to a name if the woman was right for the role. I think they (the boys, Stoddard and Blanche) would like me to let them have it for off-Broadway. So where are we?

December 5

Stopped at Blanche's yesterday. We rehashed the whole business. I said that most playwrights, by their own weakness, encourage the worst instincts of those who run Broadway. Consequently, when a writer does cling to his vision, he is derided for what is really commendable: integrity and courage are called obstinancy and self-indulgence.

December 10

No word on *Roses* in a week or so. I will not call Blanche —in fact I have no desire to.

December 11

Blanche spoke to Stoddard, who is going to ask me to do the play off-Broadway. Blanche sounded me out on this. I said no.

December 12

Ruth told me Blanche had called—asked her to pass on the following: Stoddard and Gottlieb agree the play should be done off-Broadway. They will offer the part to Albertson first. Uptown is out, as far as they're concerned. I put off calling Blanche till today to give myself a chance to really examine their offer. I did so, and concluded that if I go with them now, I would be doing it against my deepest intuitions, and out of weakness, because I have no other immediate prospects and am hungry for a bit of attention. I'll be calling Blanche in a few minutes, to say no as politely and as unequivocally as possible. What happens to *Roses* after today, I don't know.

December 13

Called Blanche—told her my decision. I felt an immediate relief—a surge of confidence.

December 18

Call from Dick Altman. David Black is hot to do *Roses* uptown and with Albertson. Would I go with him? I said yes, but that I would make no move until Jack was actually signed. When that's done, we'll start talking. Black will be told this upon his return from Boston tomorrow. Stoddard called to suggest the Arizona tryout again. I said no.

December 21

Letter from Stoddard saying she still hoped to find the means of getting *Roses* on. Called Blanche to invite her New Year's Day. She said Irene Selznick called about *Roses*. Said she'd read it, liked it. I didn't catch the outcome of their talk. Black, judging by Blanche's interpretation of Dick's words, doesn't sound all that fired up to go.

27

December 22

Met Dick at Blanche's. He said the Black thing was still alive, and that there were two other possibilities: Irene Selznick and some other party whose name escapes me, and on, and on, and on.

December 24

Dick called to say that Black was definitely out of the picture. He can't do it with Albertson.

December 27

Irene Selznick sent Blanche a copy of the fan letter she sent me about *Plowboy*. Evidently, she really does want to meet me about *Roses*. We'll set it up after the first.

January 3, 1964

Irene Selznick would want changes in the play, and doesn't know Albertson. She passed this on, lest I come in to see her, thinking she was ready to go. I appreciate that. It saves me a trip.

January 13

Blanche called to say that Haila Stoddard called on Saturday, and has a way of doing the play as I want. Blanche suggested she write all the conditions to me, rather than have me get them second-hand.

January 16

Haila's proposition: she wants to open the play in Denver at a theatre owned by Bonfils.

January 18

Called Blanche to say I wouldn't take the Denver offer.

January 28

Blanche called yesterday morning to say that there was an item in the *Times* announcing the closing of the Phoenix Theatre's current play, and cancellation of the one scheduled for March. They appear open and she wanted to call T. and suggest *Roses*. The thought of coming to roost at the Phoenix after all this time has been in my mind. I like the idea of March, with the Fair opening. Also, I like coming in on the heels of four flops. I said OK—call T. and sound him out.

January 31
The Phoenix is taking on a repertory company, so that closes it to *Roses* for now.

February 11, 1964
Ulu called—was to show *Roses* to someone.

February 12
Blanche said Haila Stoddard still calls about *Roses*. I rule out any summer theatre tryout. Not enough rehearsal time, and the wrong audience for an initial testing.

February 16
Ulu got an enthusiastic reaction to *Roses* from a guy named Hyams, who I gather is going to call me. Ulu did not mention Albertson's name to him.

February 19
Nicholas Hyams called. He and a Julian Cohen are driving here tomorrow at noon to speak of *Roses*. That they would volunteer to drive up pleases me—demonstrates at least an initial seriousness of intention. It would certainly be fine timing to have something happen before I leave for the Coast. I could use the lift.

February 20
Ulu called. He said it was just possible that Hyams and Cohen (who will arrive here at noon) could get the money, but he wasn't positive. He's told them that I will do no rewrites now, and that I have an actor set for one of the parts. I asked Ulu if they acknowledged him as the director. He said it was in the air, but not explicitly stated. I told him that I would proceed on the assumption that he is to be the director.

February 21

Blanche called yesterday morning to say that a Roger
Muchnick had obtained a copy of *Roses* and wanted to
do it now—off-Broadway. His associate is a George Ross.
They have a director in mind. Was I interested? I said I'd
call her after the meeting with Hyams and Cohen. Hyams
and Cohen arrived at one. They are sorely tempted to do
the play, but fear it is too risky for a first uptown venture.
I told them that I wasn't interested in an option—but
would (if I felt they were serious about production) give
them a free two-week to a month hold on the play—at the
end of which they must say go or no. I didn't feel they
were that serious, and they agreed. *Roses* is like a diamond
lying in plain view on the street: no one picks it up because each assumes that if it were of real value, someone
would have grabbed it before this.

February 22

I met Ulu at the Actors Studio. Told him of my scheduled meeting with Muchnick and Ross. He didn't know
either one. I said I'd call him afterward to make a supper
date so we could have a hard talk about *Roses* before I
left for the Coast this Sunday. I arrived at Blanche's a
little after four. Ross and Muchnick were there. They, in
reasonable and plain terms, outlined an off-Broadway production that would cost $5,000! I told them they were
offering me nothing I couldn't duplicate elsewhere. I said
that I'd anticipated they were going to estimate their production at fifteen to twenty thousand and I was then going
to tell them why I thought it was foolish to throw that
much away on off-Broadway, when for not so much more
they could do it uptown, and have a chance at the jackpot.
I outlined my feelings about the play, and Broadway,
didn't minimize the gamble, said it was foolish to seek
names for this when it was obvious that the play would be

the star. So why not get the best people, open as cheaply as possible, and gamble all on the reviews. Ross, when I concluded, said, "Mr. Gilroy has sold me. If I had the requisite funds, I'd write a check now." They were seriously fired up, but did not pretend the money was close at hand. They agree to Jack Albertson, and to Ulu as director. To make it short, I, feeling they were serious, have given them the play for a month (February 21–March 21). Within that time, they must call me and say yes or no. And so we parted. Even if they can't do it, I, in "selling" them, resold myself. If they pass, I shall repeat that speech until I hit a money man. And then we're off. I met Ulu at Downey's at seven. Told him all that had happened.

February 25—Hollywood

Spoke to Jack Albertson yesterday. A nice chat. He's still eager to do *Roses* and free now except for a pilot he did last fall that shows no signs of life. He favored the idea of a tryout such as Haila Stoddard suggested, and even suggested doing it in a workshop here. I told him my feelings about such tryouts. I think he thinks I'm crazy—but since it's to his advantage, he doesn't say so. It's been bubbling in me that now, this spring, is the time for *Roses*. To let $25,000 or so stop us is ridiculous. I called Ulu and told him the above. He, with genuine fire, concurs. I suggested he get an estimate on the bedrock cost of doing *Roses* on Broadway. He is going to Gene Wolsk. If it is around $25,000, and Ross and Muchnick don't come through, we're going to do it ourselves and invite Gene in.

February 26—Hollywood

I called Ruth. She objects to my getting involved with the production end of *Roses* (the money-raising, particularly). But I am determined to overrule her here. I've got the dice, and I sense they're hot, and I'm going all the way if I can.

February 28—Hollywood

Ruth said Ulu called yesterday—said he'd been unable to reach me on the phone—was going away, and would call me either today or tomorrow. He said he and Gene Wolsk see $35,000 as the bedrock minimum budget for *Roses*. Now why, I wonder, is he making himself unavailable to me for two days? Is he afraid I might fire him up again? There is something curious about his action, says my antenna.

February 29—Hollywood

I am anxious to get Ulu's call. I want to know the extent of his enthusiasm for getting *Roses* on this spring.

March 1, 1964—Hollywood

The Harmons had a party for me last night. Jack Albertson and his wife Wally were there. I told Jack the situation. He's ready to go. WHY THE HELL DOESN'T ULU CALL?

March 2—Hollywood

Called Ulu. He said he was about to call me—was waiting for 6:00 P.M. and the low rates. Thirty-five thousand to open *Roses* presumes a theatre obtained without posting bonds. Gene Wolsk not interested in doing the play. Ulu is going to try and line up a producer (in case Ross and Muchnick fall through) who can jump now with as much money as possible—the rest to be obtained by us, me primarily. Ulu will call me at six tonight. Every little while my courage or will deserts me: it seems an impossible thing for me to get *Roses* on in this fashion. I get an urge to drop it all. But then something catches hold and my determination returns.

March 3—Hollywood

Phoned Blanche. Asked her to contact Ross and Muchnick and find out how much they've raised. Told her I felt I could get some money out here, but wanted to know how much was needed before I started looking. She phoned back to say she spoke to Ross, who had apparently not really done anything concrete, but felt certain they could raise about half of the $35,000 in a month. I told Blanche that was too vague an estimate for me to proceed on—could he be more explicit? Blanche called again. Ross was not really certain about what he could raise, and didn't want me to think he was—but they did want time to try some more. Blanche told me how hard it is to raise money, etc. But something in me will not be deterred. I lunched with Jack Albertson and Joe Strick. Joe, who has read *Roses*, and likes it, thinks Jack is an inspired idea for the part. The more time I spend with Jack the more I feel he will be just right. A telegram from Blanche: "MUCHNICK JUST PHONED SAYING HE WOULD HAVE ANSWER TOMORROW FROM ONE INVESTOR GAVE PLAY." Now what does that mean? That there is one man who might put up all, or most, of the money needed? Or what? I told George Englund the status of the play; he said when I knew how much was needed, he might be able to help me.

March 4—Hollywood

Ulu called at six-fifteen. He'd spoken to Blanche. The telegram meant just one investor. Not someone who could put up all the dough. So why the wire?

March 5—Hollywood

Blanche called. Muchnick and Ross require a star in the man's role to raise money. Where have I heard that song before? They claim I didn't make it clear that Jack Albertson was a must. I think I did. Well, in any case, they have, by that request, forfeited their hold on the play. So here we go again. Called Ulu—told him the new developments. I met Palmer Thompson at four. Told him the latest about the play. Without a moment's hesitation, and without solicitation, he said, "Count on a thousand from me," and

33

that without having read the play. He said if he wasn't involved in raising money for his own project, he'd give me five grand.

March 6—Hollywood

I had breakfast with Palmer yesterday morning. I was just about decided to try and raise the $35,000 on my own. I had a pledge from David Harmon and Palmer for a grand each. If I could find 33 others who would do the same, I was home. My thought was (and is) to take pledges (solid ones) and when they total 35 Gs to call them all in and roll. Something in me still fought the idea, until I realized I wasn't asking anyone to do anything for me that I wouldn't do for them. On an impulse I went into Hemphill Noyes to see Hal Fimberg, who was my stockbroker when I lived out here. I told him I was there on business— told him the situation. "Count me in for a thousand," he said. Never asked to read the play or anything else. I could have kissed him. I wrote his name under David's and Palmer's in the back of my address book. I met Joe Strick at the Derby. The talk got around to *Roses*. I told him of my decision to raise the money myself. He offered me $1,000. I wasn't prepared for that—told him I felt funny about accepting it since we'd just met. He said, "It would be an honor to invest in that play." I accepted his pledge. Of course I was touched by it. Jack Albertson called. I told him of my decision to raise the money on my own. He started to tell me what expenses he'd need in New York. I said I felt that was a bit premature—that when the time came, I was sure such matters could be easily settled. I called Ulu—told him what I was doing. He'll try the same thing there: getting pledges for specific sums that will be delivered immediately when the grand total is 35 Gs. Ulu reminded me there would be $8,000 for returnable bonds needed in addition to the $35,000. For that I can put up my house at the lake as collateral in an emergency. Called Ruth. She was upset by my raising the money—and angry about my going to some of our friends. Why should one be reluctant to ask a friend for money? What is so sacred about money? And if friends can't encourage one another's dreams, what is the point of friendship? She advised me to get off the soapbox. What will today bring? I feel I'm on the right track. I may be going about the money-raising in a foolish way—but whatever change in me the effort itself reflects, I feel will be ultimately beneficial. I will no longer try to alter Ruth's feelings about it. It's an area of our lives where my decisions must prevail.

March 7—Hollywood

Called Alvin Ganzer for *Roses* money. Barely accomplished the preamble when he volunteered $1,000. I've had some refusals—several of them quite surprising. But a response like Alvin's gives me a real lift. I have $5,000 firmly pledged. No word from Ulu.

March 9—Hollywood

Tige Andrews loves *Roses*—was genuinely touched by it, and would like to produce it himself. He's going to beat the brush for dough this week. What a strange combination we would be. It appeals to me. If the play doesn't happen, I shall still feel this trip a great success. I am through waiting for other people to implement my dreams.

March 10—Hollywood

John Gay pledged $1,000. I now have seven grand. Flying home tomorrow.

March 12—Home

Ulu called. He hasn't been able to raise a penny so far. I told him I was going to contact Edgar Lansbury, as a possible designer, producer and/or investor. I called Ed Lansbury—told him the situation. I said I'd have a script delivered to his house. Since time was urgent, I said I'd appreciate a quick reaction. If he was interested, we would talk in detail then. I'm meeting Ulu today. I want to go over the budget very closely. I feel this great focus of purpose. I think Ulu is distressed by it—by a writer behaving so. Think he feels it sabotages my creativity.

March 13

Saw Blanche yesterday. Told her all about the play and my money-raising efforts. She volunteered a grand. I was moved. Met Ulu. We went over the budget. A lot of it still vague. Ulu seems imbued with the proper spirit of adventure. We agreed the thing we most need is a general manager who will give the budget a reality, and prepare the agenda of steps to production. He suggested, and I concurred, that we owed it to Gene Wolsk to offer the job to him. *But,* Gene must be told what we expect, since the project is such a risk: namely, complete attention and an aggressive gambler's approach. Ulu said he'd lay it on the line to Gene—and make no effort to sell it to him, as much as we both like him. Ulu mentioned Joe Beruh as another manager possibility. I met Joe Beruh at "Beebee's" opening. He seemed sufficiently driving for our purpose—and Ulu vouches for his honesty. I left Ulu with the feeling that we were in true partnership on the project and in agreement about the spirit that must be requisite in all hands if we are to succeed. Ed Lansbury called. Likes the play—is excited by our plans. He asks for three days to mull things over. I said fine. Expect to hear from him by Sunday night. Ulu called. Gene can't give us his full time, so he's out. Gene suggested Leonard Soloway for a manager. I'm sure Leonard would not accept. It would be like being offered the best man's role at the wedding of a girl you'd courted for years. Joe Beruh has done only one uptown show. I think that's a plus. He might not be so brainwashed. Ulu is approaching Joe. I'm suspending the money quest till we can sit down with a general manager. I now have nine grand pledged—twenty-six to go. I figure I have about three weeks in which to do it, if we're going to go this spring.

March 14

Ulu called last night. He's contacted Joe Beruh, who's read the play and likes it. Joe thinks we can pull it off at around thirty-five grand. He grasps the spirit of the venture. Ulu says he looks like our man. I feel he's right. We three will meet at Jack Delaney's at five o'clock today. Joe will have worked on the budget by then. Also, Joe gave Edgar Lansbury, with whom he's worked, a big recommendation. This impressed Ulu, and so helps to tie us together a bit more. Now if Ed will only come in with us. Of course, there is still the matter of $26,000 to be raised. But if all other systems are go, I shall accomplish that!

March 15

Wasn't sure I'd recognize Joe Beruh, but spotted him approaching Delaney's. Hailed him. We chatted a bit over a drink until Ulu arrived. Joe does have the proper spirit—seems to delight in a low-budget production—welcomes the challenge. His figures come to this: $40,000 overall—of which $10,000 goes for bonds and reserve. And in the thirty grand there seems to be some slack for emergency. Joe is going after a theatre on Monday—going to the Shuberts to see what sort of a bargain he might strike. Joe will mail me a budget breakdown. I await Edgar Lansbury's decision anxiously. I'll contact John Fernbach tomorrow. Try to interest him in our adventure. He might just come along. I think what we're doing has an instinctive appeal for many people. Ulu and I are increasingly determined to bring this off.

March 16

Edgar Lansbury called. "All things being equal, you've got yourself a designer and a producer," he said. I responded enthusiastically. He said Joe Beruh was "a good man." Ulu and I are meeting Ed at his home at two-thirty today. I'm meeting Ulu at one for lunch. It all begins to sound most promising.

March 17

Went to Blanche's—briefed her on where things stood—told her I was meeting Edgar, who was coming in as designer and producer, though I didn't know to what extent. She was a trifle pessimistic, but I was in orbit. She said she'd approached a few people for money without success. I said, "I feel sorry for those people because they'll miss out on our opening night party." Ulu and I lunched in the Grill Room at the Taft. We discussed casting, and what we hoped for from the meeting with Ed. I was a bit apprehensive about how Ed and Ulu might get on. They are such opposite types. Of course they do have one thing in common—a basic decency. We took a cab to Ed's. Apartment 13B—my lucky number. Ulu was a bit nervous. He had refrained from a drink at lunch—said it would make him drowsy. Ulu, Ed and I settled down to a nice talk. General conversation. I could feel them liking each other. No bull or pretense on either side. No contesting. They recognized and responded to that mutual decency mentioned earlier. I am going to guarantee to raise $15,000. Ed guarantees $25,000, which he may raise alone or with someone else. We looked through casting books. I could feel us all in agreement as to the sort of people we want. Ulu liked the picture of Albertson—was heartened by his appearance. We agreed that the thing most immediately needed was a lawyer. I called John Fernbach. He was in a meeting. Ulu, Ed and I had a drink, more good and welding talk, and parted in the glow of a happy adventure felicitously begun. Both Ed and Ulu were going to approach lawyers in case Fernbach was not available, or was too costly. We agreed that we should try to cinch a lawyer by tonight. Ulu went out of the room. Ed told me he liked him. Ulu, on the way downtown, said the same thing about Ed. I called Fernbach at his home last evening. I told him our situation. I made a date for Ed and me to meet him at his office at four-thirty today. I notified Ed, who is setting up an appointment with another lawyer prior to that. I called Jack Albertson to alert him. He wasn't in. I left word I'd call today—said to tell him "things look good." I feel quite drained this morning and there is still so much to do before the real work (rehearsals) begins.

March 18

Went to Fernbach's office. Edgar was in the waiting room. I gave him the budget Joe Beruh had sent to me. Ed and I were really there to shop, but John Fernbach took the bit in his mouth and was working on our situation before we were there five minutes. I could see that Ed was impressed with John's manner and spirit, so I didn't try to slow him down. I suggested $1,000, plus $100 a week—much below their usual fee. John generously agreed. This cinched it. Frank Weissburg (John's associate and an expert on SEC dealings of this sort) came in. He is going right to work to try to get us the necessary clearance as quickly as possible. In filing with the SEC we must include a summary of our personal activities over the past five years—and a hundred-word synopsis of the play. John took down other information: The director's fee, at minimum, is $2,000 plus 1 percent. We put Ulu in at the $2,000, and $1\frac{1}{2}$ percent. I now feel a bit guilty for committing Ulu without consulting him. I'm sure the figures are agreeable, since we're all taking minimum, but I could have gone about it more diplomatically. We left Fernbach. Ed canceled the appointment with the other lawyer we were considering. We now had a producer, director, scene designer, lawyer, general manager and one actor. Joe Beruh will be both a general manager and company manager. I dined at the Lansburys'. After supper, Ed and I prepared the résumés required by the SEC—and I did the play synopsis. Feeling comfortable, after a couple of drinks and several glasses of wine, we went to the Oak Room bar at the Plaza to meet Joe Beruh. We brought Joe up to date. He and Ed went over the budget in detail. They are in tune. Joe suggested possible economies that Ed responded to—one is the possibility of building the set on the stage. Joe is going to press his theatre quest. Fernbach has a contract on his desk for *Roar Like a Dove,* due at the Booth in May—bonds for the theatre are $10,000. We want to pay no more than $3,000. I called Jack Albertson, told him we have every chance of going into rehearsal by mid-April. He said he'd keep his time clear. Am I overly solicitous of Jack because he is the father? Am I trying to do something for him that I never had the chance to do for my own father? Joe, Ed and I parted in good spirits at eleven-thirty.

March 19

I felt sufficiently guilty about settling Ulu's fee (without consulting him) to call and say so. He was out. I told Rose how I felt. Ed Lansbury called to say he'd dropped the required papers at John Fernbach's office. Ed's initially going to try to raise his money in big chunks from a few people. I hope he hasn't overestimated what he can raise. I suspect not. He repeated to me what he'd mentioned the night before—that he didn't particularly care for the play's title—asked what I felt about that. I told him I'd lived with the title for two years and was quite satisfied with it. I soft-pedaled there: actually I think it's a great title. I did let him know that I was firmly wedded to it—said that his was the first objection I'd had. He seemed to bow to that. Ulu called. Rose had given him my message about his fee. He told me not to concern myself. He is drawing up a list of actresses and actors we might conceivably want for the mother and son roles. About a day or so ago Ruth said (I don't know what it was apropos of) that she saw the play going on this spring—but minus Jack Albertson, a curious intuition. I plan to go to the city tomorrow, resume my money quest, and see Ulu and Ed if possible.

March 21

Called Ulu. He said he and Edgar would meet me at Blanche's at twelve-thirty. Blanche canceled a hair appointment so she would be present to receive them. Since there was time to kill I decided to try to raise more money by phone. I called Jerry Perenchio. I barely stated the purpose of the call when he said, "You've got a grand, now what else is new?" He even volunteered an overcall, which I refused. I said I felt it was an invitation to laxity. I called Jim McLaughlin. I let him know that I would not recommend this as a sound investment to anyone—told him we wanted no "tough" money involved. If we hit, fine, but if one were primarily interested in financial return, then this was not the investment for them. Jim asked for a day to think it over. Edgar and Ulu arrived. I told Ed I now had $10,000, and asked if he was having any luck. He said yes most confidently—but volunteered no figure. The three of us, and Blanche, settled down to a discussion of casting. Ulu gave us each a list of all the possibilities he could conceive for the mother's role, which we agreed was our most pressing need. Going down the list, we eliminated anyone that any of the three of us had a flat-out objection to. Certain names we left open. Others we grouped under a preferred heading. There was an easy give-and-take in all this—an intuitive bowing to each other's judgments at certain moments: THAT RIGHT AIR PREVAILED. I'm sure Blanche felt it. Now, a wonderful thing—a most significant thing to the overall project—occurred. Jan Sterling's name came up. I said I'd seen her in the O'Casey readings at UCLA, and liked her very much. Also, that I was told a year ago that she'd read *Roses* and was interested in doing it at that time. Ulu has no clear picture of her. Ed had worked with her—liked her personally, but had an objection that he couldn't articulate. Since his objection was vague, we (at his suggestion) did not scratch her name, and proceeded to other women. In some way her name came back into our talk. Ed now remembered that he'd seen her in a play last year. The play was a disaster (he left after the first act), but he (and the critics) liked *her* very much. Then came the moment that augurs so well: Ed, with no urging, reversed himself on Jan Sterling— suddenly saw her a new way—was excited by the idea of her in this role, and did not hesitate to say so—insisted that she go to the head of the list. I agreed, and Ulu was open. Edgar is going to contact her and, if she's in the East, set up a meeting if possible. Ulu is going to keep searching for boys. We have no objection to "discovering" someone. I took Ed and Ulu to Whyte's for lunch. We had a feeling of accomplishment. Here is how things stand: Frank Weissburg pursues the SEC business; Joe Beruh is out after a theatre and reportedly confident; Ulu and Ed are going to meet, alone, to discuss the set in a general way; on Tuesday I am coming in to meet Ed, Joe and a prospective press agent, recommended by Joe. I hope to meet Jan Sterling that day—and I plan to take Ed and Ulu to the Bronx to expose them to the real setting, for whatever it's worth. As we parted, Ed said, "I hope our present feeling will continue throughout the project." We are all a little embarrassed by the generous spirit that envelops the venture—and afraid it might vanish. But I really don't think it will vanish. Jim McLaughlin called last night to say he'd invest $1,000. I have $11,000 now, and $4,000 to go.

March 23

Blanche called to say that Maude Franchot liked *Roses* and was interested in a coproduction deal with Ed. Blanche called Ed on Saturday, and he said he'd take a budget to Maude. Ruth is won to the project now that Ed is producing.

March 24

I called Edgar last evening—was relieved to hear that Ulu was there discussing the set. Not having heard from them since Friday, I feared things were slowing down. Ed called back later. I am to meet him and Ulu today at noon. I'll take them to my old neighborhood in the Bronx. From there we'll go to meet Joe Beruh.

March 25

Arrived in the city about 11:30 A.M. Took a cab to the Filmways studio at 127th Street. Edgar introduced me to Kenny Utt, an associate of his on The Defenders. We'd met years ago on Studio One. He'd read *Roses* and was most enthusiastic about it—is one of Ed's investors. Ed said that in their discussion of the set, Ulu had mentioned his feeling that the furniture should have a somewhat cold and formal air. I concurred. Ed noted that much of the play happens in the kitchen—said he might hold to that, and reserve the living room for special moments. I like that too. Ulu arrived. We went in Ed's station wagon to the Bronx. It was exciting for me to make this trip—the fulfillment of some dream. We double-parked on a street near my Aunt Clemie's. We walked up University Avenue to 176th Street. I pointed out the candy store, P.S. 82, the Park Plaza Theatre, etc. We walked up 176th

43

Street to good old 116. Ulu regarded the building with a
darting intensity that drew the attention of passers-by.
We entered the apartment house. Quite shabby now.
Gone, that elaborate glass chandelier that hung in the
entrance hall—replaced by a naked neon coil. The walls
coated with a hideous orange-brown paint. I tried Mrs.
Moses' bell (2E)—no answer. I tried Mrs. Frieman (3E)
—no answer. I rang 4E (which was our apartment). A
woman came to the peephole. I told her I used to live there
—that I was a writer—that the gentlemen with me were
producing a play of mine which took place in that apartment and that I'd very much like to show it to them. How
bizarre my story must have sounded! But apparently it
made some impression, for the woman now appeared at
the chained door. She was tempted to let us in, but apprehensive. A lady living on the floor above went by. The
lady in 4E told her the situation. The other lady did not
comprehend—thought I was trying to get the apartment
back. Out of this confusion, and thanks to the courage of
Mrs. Gannon (the woman in 4E), we gained admission
to the apartment. As she ushered us in, she said, "I hope
you're what you say you are." As we left, she said, "I was
never to a stage play in my life—could you send me a
couple of tickets?" I assured her we would. We went to
my aunt's house—had a drink with her and my Uncle
Frank. We drove to Sardi's. Ulu left us. Ed and I went in
to meet Joe Beruh and Max Eisen. Before their arrival, Ed
gave me a copy of the proposed budget, estimated weekly
budget, and a memo from Joe on the availability of certain
theatres. Joe and Max Eisen arrived. We hired Max as our
press agent. Some talk of our pre-opening campaign. I'm
bringing my *Plowboy* scrapbook in tomorrow. When Max
digests it we'll plan the approach. I gather from Ed that
he has seven thousand in hand and feelers out for the rest.

44

He would welcome a coproducer eagerly, which worries me just a tic. But he seems so confident that he will have the money in time that I must go along with him. He still has not reached Jan Sterling—says he will by tomorrow.

March 26

Ed got a script to Jan Sterling. She claims no prior knowledge of the play. Ed says Joe is no longer confident about getting a theatre for three grand. Ed called again later to say he'd been at Fernbach's to sign papers and certain of the contracts. I have to be there before 10:00 A.M. today to do the same.

March 27

Arrived in city at nine forty-five yesterday. To Fernbach's. Frank Weissburg and Richard Blumenthal attended me. I read and signed contracts: the one between Ed and me as general partners; my contract as author; Ulu's contract; another contract whose title I can't recall. I also read the offering circular that the SEC will have to approve—and signed the document that accompanies it. Fernbach arrived and entered the proceedings. I felt well taken care of. I went to Max Eisen's. His office is in the Sardi Building, which reminds me of a rabbit warren. Joe Beruh was present. Both he and Max were impressed by the *Plowboy* clips—and agreed that I was the focal point for publicity. I made it clear that we wanted no rover-boy stuff—or heralding of a shoe-string operation. If the reviews are good— then we will announce cost. We want a dignified campaign; no announcements until all contracts are signed; and nothing sent out without Edgar's and my approval. They agreed. They'll digest the material and mull a campaign. Went to the Actors Studio to see *The Birthday*, a new play by William Snyder, directed by Ulu. I called Ed after the performance—told him I was now certain we were in good directorial hands. Ed said he called Jan Sterling, she was halfway through *Roses,* and "loving it." I told Ed I was going to call Jack Albertson. Felt it was time to talk price with him. Ed agreed. We decided to offer him the customary minimum during the four-week rehearsal; round-trip plane fare; $150 a week expenses during rehearsal; a starting salary of $600 a week; and my word that if we prospered he would share equitably. I called Jack—presented the above. He responded negatively: began to tell me about his financial plight and how actors were always getting the short end, etc., etc. I had somehow anticipated this, but was still disappointed. I took it upon myself to raise our offer from $600 to $750 a week. He was still unhappy. I told him to think on the deal overnight and call me today. If he turns us down it will be a stunning twist in the log of this journey. I am glad I handled this rather than leaving it to Joe Beruh. If it falls through I will know why, and not be inclined to blame intermediaries.

March 28

I called Ed. Told him of my talk with Jack—alerted him to the possibility that we might have to get another actor for the father's role. He called back later to say that Jan Sterling liked *Roses* very much but can't meet us till Monday. Jack Albertson called at eleven last night. I felt he wanted to say yes (will ultimately say it) but was looking for me to coax him: I made it clear that I wanted him but that the play was going on with or without him. He said his agent felt it was a good deal for him, career-wise, and so did Wally. I advised him to reflect another day and call with his decision tonight. He will do this.

March 29

Jack called last night. It's a deal! Of course there will be such matters as length of contract to be worked out by Joe and Jack's agent. When I stop and reflect on the enormity of all that must be done in the next few weeks, I am staggered. Fortunately there is not much time for reflection. In bed last night I played *Roses* through with emphasis on Jack's scenes. I am now certain that he is going to be fine.

March 30

I await word from Ed about our meeting with Jan Sterling, tentatively scheduled for today. A bad intuition about the play tickles the back of my head—or is it just fatigue?

March 31

Ed called at noon yesterday to say we would meet Jan Sterling at his apartment at five. I got to the city about three. Went to Blanche's—chatted with her for about an hour. She admitted that she never thought we'd get this far in the venture. Went to Ed's. Jan Sterling arrived. She was most candid in her enthusiasm for the part—allowed that money (Ed had mentioned our tight budget) would be no obstacle. Ulu quizzed her about her background—seemed to be in contact with her. We told her to keep the script. Ulu is lunching with her on Wednesday. All things considered, I said (after she left) that I would gamble on her. Ed felt similarly inclined, though not so definitely. Ulu was more reluctant. They were going to check on Stanley, Page, Hunter and Wright today—because we must make a decision by the end of the week. I suspect Jan will get the part. She is, by her own admission, not physically ideal—or at least it does not seem so now. But I think it can work. My intuition says go—but if Ulu doesn't feel she is right after tomorrow's meeting, we will look elsewhere. Of course I would take Page or Stanley—but I think the thought of getting them is a pipe dream. Joe Beruh arrived. We went over the budget. We added $2,000 more to theatre bonds. He let us know that in exchange for investing their fees in the play, he and Max would expect a piece of the producers' share.

April 1, 1964

Joe Beruh called last night. He just had a "tough session" with Jack and his agent. They want $750 a week for openers, with subsequent raises clearly defined. I told Joe their requests were all right with me—said if Edgar agreed he could send them the letter spelling the deal. Ulu called. He hears *Three Sisters* is on again. Which rules out Page and Stanley. He's meeting Sterling today. I told him to be sure and check on her willingness to alter her hair color—with a wig or otherwise.

April 2

Called Ulu. He'd lunched with Jan Sterling. He enjoyed it; likes her personally, but came away more convinced that she is not right for this part. We are contacting other actresses. Kim Hunter is reading the play now. Teresa Wright again expressed a lack of enthusiasm for the part.

April 3

I was late getting to Blanche's, where we were to meet candidates for the boy's role. Of the boys seen yesterday, Martin Sheen was the standout. He is not as good-looking or as delicate as one might like, but he has the energy and command that we need. I was most impressed with him. We are going to see him in *Pretzel Factory* tomorrow. I suspect he's our boy, but we'll see many more and will work them on a stage before deciding. The SEC clearance came through; all the forms are being printed. We'll soon be calling the money in. Meanwhile, we pursue actresses, and have engaged Michael Shurtleff to help us cast. We also have a stage manager, Paul Leaf, who has thrown in with us because he likes the script and the nature of the project. Ed seemed a bit preoccupied all day. I said he looked like a man with problems. He said it was just fatigue. Leonard Soloway called Blanche—told her Joe

Beruh had approached the Osterman office about a theatre. He (Leonard) said he would be as helpful as possible. I thought this was nice of him, and after consulting Ed, called Leonard back and said if he wanted to coproduce with Ed, he could share the credit for $10,000. He seemed doubtful, but thanked me for the invitation. I wonder what Ed's money situation is. Bob Ehrenbard met me at Blanche's and drove to our house. Lila and the boys had driven up earlier in the day. Bob said he and Lila had talked it over, and insisted on investing $500 in the play. I was most grateful. That means I have $11,500. Jack Albertson called. I told him we agreed to his conditions. He asked for a one-day trip to the Coast—I mean, he asked for the time—either April 26 or 27 to do retakes on a film. He assured me it would be only one day, so I agreed. He was most amiable—said we could count on financial assistance from him if we get in a tight spot after the opening.

April 5

I called Ulu to see what had transpired on Friday, and to see where and when we were to meet before the *Pretzel Factory* matinee. Ulu said Kim Hunter was having her agent read the play over the weekend. There was not much new about the mother's role beyond that. He said we were going to interview twenty-five more boys on Tuesday and then have the "finalists" work on stage on Thursday. He quoted Mike Shurtleff as saying that he could not render much casting aid in the woman area since we'd thought of just about everyone he would suggest. I questioned the sense of spending two more days on boys when we had Martin Sheen in our pocket. I felt we might better use those days in pursuit of a mother. Ulu felt we should continue canvassing for boys while simultaneously pressing the mother search. Ed Lansbury called. He was of the same mind as Ulu. Felt we should take as much time as possible before locking things up. He agreed to giving Jack Albertson the day he requested for retakes in Hollywood. Driving into the city I felt that surge of joy about our prospects—that rush of confidence that seems to attend all the successful things I've been involved in. I realized, even as these good feelings flooded me, that I would know many equally dark moments before this venture was over, but that that good feeling would still be my basic one. I sang as I drove. Ulu and Ed and Ed's mother (Moina McGill) met me at the Steuben Tavern at twelve-thirty. Ed gave me the offering circulars and limited partnership agreements, which make it possible to call in money. Ed had given a script to Judy Holliday. We then went to *Pretzel Factory* at the Eugene O'Neill Theatre, which we have a chance of getting. It is a bit larger than we would like—but excellent in all other respects. "I'll take it," I said. Ed said to Ulu that "they must combine to hold me down." AND RIGHT THEY ARE! The play began. Only Ulu saw the end. Ed left after Act One, I went after Act Two. Everyone, including Martin, looked terrible. No wonder his agent didn't want us to see it. I don't preclude the possibility that Martin may be fine for us, but now he will have to demonstrate his capacity onstage to win the role. We were all discouraged by the experience. I felt very bad—and angered at myself because I had approved him prematurely. I must learn to withhold judgment until all the evidence that can be obtained is in. As Ruth said later, I must get over this aversion to shopping—which makes me take a house, or a car, or an actor on first impulse. I could see Ulu and Ed thinking, "My God, if he was ready to accept Sterling and Sheen on such flimsy evidence, how do we know that he wasn't dead wrong about Albertson?" I came away with my confidence (temporarily) shaken in my own judgment. I told Ulu to tell Ed, whom he is seeing today about the set, that I am not locked in on Martin Sheen. I wanted to call

Ed (who seemed so glum when he left us) and apologize for my impulsiveness. But I sensed that to make such a call would only be another impulsive act. I think I have finally learned my lesson—and cheaply, at that. I called Harry Keller. He said to put him in for a grand. I called Art Silver, he said the same. I now have $13,500 confirmed. Harry called back to ask if Paul Gilbert (his business manager), who was at his house, could invest a grand. I said yes. Spoke to Paul and thanked him. That puts me at $14,500. Must mail out the forms, to get the money coming in, today.

April 7

Went to Blanche's yesterday. Gave her the limited partnership agreement form on *Roses*. To Downey's to meet Ulu. He was a bit anxious because Kim Hunter wants to do *Roses*, and her agent was pressing Ed for an immediate deal. It seems she was on the verge of signing a contract for another engagement, and couldn't stall a decision. Ulu wanted to meet her, and then have us meet her before deciding. I agreed. Ulu feared Ed was succumbing to the agent's pressure. I assured Ulu no deal would be consummated until she had been interviewed. I spoke to Ed, who was discussing price with Kim's agent. We agreed that if price were mutually agreeable it would only be the prelude to meeting her. I read the play last night for the first time in a year or so. I see Jack beautifully and I see Martin Sheen—the mother is Geraldine Page, if we only had her. Must run. We begin to see boys at Blanche's at ten-thirty tomorrow morning.

April 8

Arrived at Blanche's at ten-fifteen. Ulu came at ten-twenty—and then Ed arrived. A fellow named Allan Hopkins (a production assistant) volunteered to assist Ulu for the day. He met the boys at the door, ushered them in,

accomplished introductions and took pertinent information. We saw some twenty-five boys between ten-thirty and
six. Had sandwiches sent in: the saltiest lox I've ever had.
Mike Shurtleff was responsible for many of the boys—and
they were a much more rewarding group than the bunch
we saw the other day. About a dozen of them were given
scripts, told certain scenes to concentrate on, and will read
for us tomorrow at the Royale Theatre. Martin Sheen
might still get the part, but I doubt it. Several boys seen
yesterday had that quality of understanding that seems
more important now that I've read the play. It might well
be that Dutch boy, whose name escapes me. Ulu handled
the interviews very nicely. A couple of times he ventured
into areas that were personal and unrelated to our purpose.
I cut off one question—about an illness that had taken the
boy home for a year. Ulu asked what the illness was. It was
obviously a breakdown of sorts, and the actor (who was
plainly not right for the part) squirmed. I advised him not
to answer; Ulu took my intrusion well. Ed left at three.
There is some question about including a piano among
the stage furnishings. I would like one if it didn't have to
be used. Ulu and Ed feel it would have to be used, so I say
eliminate it rather than try to force a moment that could
break the mood. They are thinking about it. I think Ed is
having a bit of trouble raising his part of the money; I feel
it's best not to ask. We might meet Ruth Ford for dinner
tomorrow night. Scripts went to Geraldine Fitzgerald and
Vivian Nathan. We are contacting Lee Grant and Jan
Minor. No word from Judy Holliday. The mother's role is
our big problem. We might get the Royale Theatre. I dined
with Ulu. Told him my reaction to reading the play. I
answered questions he asked. We seemed in firm agreement on procedure. Both of us came away from yesterday
with good feelings about each other strengthened. Ulu's
agent had some minor contract points. No problem there.

April 9

Ulu called last night. He sounds exhausted. Vivian Nathan said no, Ruth Ford said no. We begin with boys at the Royale at twelve-fifteen today.

April 10

Arrived in the city at a little after ten yesterday. Went to Rockefeller Center to have a photo taken that is required by the state in order to solicit funds for the play. It was a jiffy passport picture operation. The photographer asked me several times if I wanted to remove my glasses. I said no. When I picked the pictures up, I understood his insistence—I was wearing sunglasses. I had other pictures made. Went to Blanche's. George Mucha arrived. He is a Czech from Prague—a playwright who is translating *Plowboy,* which is to be done there. He looked like Eddie Rickenbacker. As he and Blanche and I taxied to the Royale Theatre, I told him he was about to be present at a most significant occasion in my life: this would be the first time that my lines would be spoken in a Broadway theatre. How I loved entering that empty theatre. No set could excite me as much as that bare stage illumined by that harsh, naked bulb. Rose Gregorio graciously volunteered to read with all the boys. We read boys from twelve-thirty until about seven. Only two of them brought the part to life . . . and those two were excellent. One was Martin Sheen, who had his scenes memorized. The other boy was a complete surprise. His name is John Karlen. We almost didn't give him a script the other day. He was superb. His understanding enveloped everything onstage. Bert Howard, who volunteered as Ulu's temporary assistant, read the father's part with some of the boys. A vigorous reader, he knocked several of them down in the physical bits. Irene Dailey, who was suggested by Joe Beruh, read for us. She made a striking impression. I wouldn't be surprised if she got the part, but it's early to say. I'm due at Blanche's at eleven today to meet three more women. Total impression of the script yesterday was most favorable and shared by all hands: saw enough sparks to know the play is a live one and playable—but difficult. Palmer Thompson called. He's decided he wants to put in $2,400 (three units) instead of $1,000. I'm overwhelmed. Ulu is shaping up very well—handled things excellently, especially in dealing with a truculent kid who came by uninvited and resented having to wait.

April 11

Arrived at Blanche's a bit before eleven. Sada Thompson appeared. She is a bit young, but seemed quite suited for the mother's role in every other way. Ulu arrived. He knows her work and thinks well of it. He made it clear that age was a problem. Since the role is not a character part, the actress would have to draw on herself, which accentuates the age matter. Ulu looked at me and I said I felt we should give her a script. I didn't mention it to anyone, but Sada Thompson resembled my mother physically. While waiting for Edgar, Ulu brought me up to date: Lee Grant said no, Colleen Dewhurst is not available, no word on Geraldine Fitzgerald. Ed arrived. Ulu and Ed went to Ed's place to work on the set plan. We all agree on no piano. After the readings yesterday we know we don't need the crutch. Joe Beruh has nailed May 28th as our opening date—but that's too near the Memorial Day holiday—we're going to try to move it up.

April 12

Ulu called. He said he was worried about getting the mother but later confesssed that Irene Dailey had made as good an impression on him as she had on me. He suggested the possibility of using a narrator at the beginning of the

54

play, which we examined and mutually discarded. He was going to have a chat with Irene Dailey—and is to see Jan Sterling today. He intends to be perfectly honest with her, which I think she will appreciate. He said that Joe Beruh told him we could have the Royale for a May 25th opening.

April 13

No contracts signed, but I'm told we definitely do have the Royale for a May 25th opening. That news made it all suddenly seem real—and frightening. Ed Lansbury called, he sounded much happier. I suspect his money is coming in. Ruth and I met Ulu and Rose at the Cookery. The boy who showed us to our table had read for us on Wednesday. He hadn't seen me at the rear of the theatre the other day. I introduced myself. He later returned to our table and said, "I may have given a lousy reading, but at least you remembered my name." Shelley Winters is reading the play on the Coast. I meet the fellows at Blanche's today at noon to see more actresses. Tomorrow we use the Royale to read.

April 14

Saw several actresses at Blanche's yesterday. All will read for us at the Royale today. Saw several boys. One we invited back today on a hunch—not a strong one. I feel certain it will be either Karlen or Sheen. Blanche brought sandwiches in for Ulu, herself and me. Paul Leaf arrived. He seemed alert and competent. He's found us a place at Fifty-first Street between Tenth and Eleventh avenues where we can rehearse free of charge. The owner of the place will do our hauling job. They (Ulu, Ed and Paul) keep talking of "portals." I'm ashamed to ask what they are—but I will. Joe Beruh arrived. He's found an artist (Jim Pearsall) who designed a symbol for the show—referred to as a "logo." It is an arresting thing—a rose with a human eye at its center. With the exception of Paul, we all responded to it. The more we looked, the more we liked it—agreed that that was it. Some dispute about when we'll move from the rehearsal hall to the Royale. Economy dictates a Monday move (May the 18th) and our first paid preview on Wednesday. Ulu fights for a Friday the 15th move to give the actors a chance to accustom themselves to the stage. Joe Beruh opposes this—says our budget can't stand it. Estimates it would cost an extra $500. We decided to postpone a decision until we are in rehearsal. Joe and Ed are opening a bank account this morning. They'll bring me signature cards. Any two of the three of us can sign checks. Will we be hung up on the time it takes the checks from California to clear? Joe Beruh called Ed Bondi at the Morris office (which is handling Jack while he is on the East Coast) to say that we wanted Jack here on the weekend. Bondi started some jazz about not letting Jack come till all bonds were posted. Joe told him they'd be posted on Friday. Max Eisen is setting up a meeting with Louis Funke of the *Times*. Called Jack Albertson. Spoke to his wife. Told her we open at the Royale on May the 25th, that rehearsals begin next Monday, April the 20th, that we'd like Jack here on Saturday the 18th, and for him to call me when he has his flight booked. She sounded happy about all this.

April 15

Arrived at the Royale at 11:30 A.M. yesterday. Raining. Entered through the stage door. I was the first to arrive. Sat alone on the stage. The house dark. I felt most comfortable and at home. George Blanchard arrived. Paul Leaf was next. Paul turned on the work light and lowered the curtain a few feet. The elderly man who guards the stage door was angry—told Paul he had no right to touch that curtain unless he was a member of Union 1. The old man said that even *he* was not authorized to lower the curtain, and that if a member of Union 1 saw the curtain was moved, there would be hell to pay. Paul said something which seemed to pacify him. To think that a curtain can't be lowered without the proper credentials! How constipated the whole thing is. We read six women, including Irene Dailey. Only Irene was interesting. I'm excited by what I feel she can do. Martin Sheen now seems our best prospect for the boy's role. Ed says he lacks between five and ten thousand dollars and is sick and tired of trying to identify Ulu Grosbard and Jack Albertson to potential investors. He agrees with me that Ulu has taken hold well. He and I meet Funke at Sardi's tomorrow. Ed is understandably anxious to get a name (who is a good actress) in the woman's part. He keeps calling Shelley Winters. At last report she was half through the script and liking it. We are reading Irene Dailey and Martin Sheen at the Orpheum tonight. Blanche was present for several hours at the Royale yesterday. She said she felt very good about the script.

April 16

Spoke to Dan Petrie, who is here for a week from Spain. He spoke highly of Martin Sheen and said nice things about Irene Dailey and Jan Sterling. Arrived at Blanche's at around 4:00 P.M., then to the Orpheum at around five-thirty. Ulu and Paul were there. Read a woman and a boy. Neither was for us. Martin Sheen and Irene Dailey arrived. Ulu had them improvise; told them to try and get to know each other. They must have gone on for a half hour. It was most interesting—the content as well as the process. Irene said she'd been on the stage for fourteen years before she'd decided to study acting—said it took three years just to break all the bad habits she'd picked up in performing. Martin has been in New York five years. Irene and Martin concluded their session. Paul and Martin and I went to Ratner's to eat while Ulu went uptown to pick up Jan Sterling. Just before going to Ratner's, Joe Beruh came in—informed me that Jack's New York agent had called to say there was a hitch in Jack's contract: they now want a clause releasing Jack for a TV series. It is a bit vague—but upsetting. I told Joe to call Bondi this morning and find out exactly what they want. Then we will proceed. In the meantime, everyone is to think of actors for the father's role, because this could be trouble. Jan Sterling volunteered to help us out by reading with Martin and doing an improvised scene with him. She is a delightful person—told Ulu that she shared his misgivings about herself in this role, but said she would do it if we couldn't get someone better suited. Jan, Martin, Ulu and I went back to Ratner's a happy group. It was the improvisation between Jan and Martin witnessed by only Ulu and me that seemed to bind us. Ulu and I walked together after putting Jan in a cab and saying good night to Martin. Ulu liked Irene's work very much. If his feeling holds this morning, and Ed agrees, we're going to sign her and Martin. Must rush now to get to Blanche's at eleven-thirty. This will be a day of decision. How do I feel? Great. Nothing is going to stop this from happening. If we lose Jack it will only be a temporary setback. Ulu shares my feeling. So let the good times roll.

April 17

Arrived at Blanche's at 11:30 A.M. yesterday. Ulu arrived next, then Ed, Paul Leaf and finally Joe Beruh, who had spoken to Bondi. Fare must be deposited with William Morris before Jack will board the plane. He will arrive Monday, the 20th; and *most* important, he wants a clause that will permit him to leave the show on June 13th (two weeks after we open) if a pending TV deal works out!!!

Bondi said he asked Jack if he were willing to blow the
deal over the June 13th thing and Jack said yes!!!! I called
Jack immediately. Told him there was no point discussing
the other items until the June 13th thing was settled.
There is a series (something to do with Bing Crosby or his
company) which goes into production on June 13th. Jack
is being considered for it. I told Jack that that was absolutely unacceptable to us. He either went with them or
with us, and we had to know that immediately. "I'll call
you tonight," he said. I told him we couldn't wait that long,
said I'd be at this number at 4:00 P.M. (1:00 P.M. his time)
and I would expect a call from him then. He would say
yes or no, and that would be final. It was all so ironic that
I felt the comedy more than the disappointment. Blanche
was gloomiest of all—kept saying that she hoped I'd learned
something from this, about trusting people, etc. Ulu was
jolted. Ed, Joe and I went to Sardi's to meet Max Eisen
and Louis Funke of the *New York Times*. I told Funke
the genesis of the play. He started telling me about *his*
father, and Max interrupted to talk of *his*. Funke said that
in all his years he had never announced a play that was
going into rehearsal so immediately. Back to Blanche's to
await Jack's call. It came at ten minutes after four. Jack
said he'd killed the other deal. I said we'd have his plane
fare posted at the Morris office today—and bonds posted at
Equity at 2:00 P.M. today. He'll fly in tomorrow and we'll
all have dinner tomorrow night. We have Martin Sheen
signed at $300 a week with raises. We're dickering with
Dailey's agent.

April 18

Met Ed and Joe Beruh at Blanche's at noon. Ed and I
each handed Joe $2,000 in cash for the Equity bonds. We
will reimburse ourselves when the checks clear. We
stopped at CBS for lunch while Ed had the set plans

duplicated free of charge—a saving of $40. To Equity to see Mr. Mayo, a short man with a littered desk. All OK there. On to the William Morris office to sign Jack's contract. On to Fernbach's. Frank Weissburg looked over the theatre contract. He called Alvin Cooperman (the Shubert manager), got the $22,000 stop figure down to $18,000. And the 70–30 to 75–25 if we hit $25,000.

April 19

Who's nervous? ME! Didn't sleep well Friday night because I had no word from Jack. Woke yesterday morning—still no word. Figured I'd wait till nine (on the chance of a telegram) before phoning him. At eight-thirty Western Union called: "ARRIVING 4:45 P.M. LOVE JACK." I felt most relieved. Notified Joe Beruh, who had volunteered to pick Jack up at the airport. Met Ulu at Blanche's at 6:00 P.M. He wanted me to read some of the play aloud to him, which I did—and enjoyed doing. He quizzed me on the background of certain points. He said again how much he loved the script—that the deeper he went into it, the more he liked it. "Chekhovian," he said. I blushed appropriately. I went to the Osborne Apartments at Fifty-seventh Street and Seventh Avenue, where Jack is renting a room from Paul Hartman. The building is eighty years old—ornate, heavy, dark. The paint seems to have accumulated on the walls like wax drippings on a wine bottle. Jack was dressing when I arrived. It is seven years since he's been in New York. He admitted an apprehension about coming back. As we walked along Fifty-seventh Street he kept searching for landmarks and was pleased whenever he spotted a building or bar that he recognized. We entered Whyte's. Edgar arrived. They got on immediately. Ulu arrived. He was most guarded and reserved—volunteered very little in conversation, but you could feel his attention never leaving Jack. I got Jack reminiscing and telling stories. We all three laughed genuinely, which seemed to relax him considerably. He is 5′11¾″ tall. Thank God. I had been worrying about his height all week—had a secret fear that I remembered him incorrectly, and that he would turn out to be 5′2″. Leaving Whyte's, Jack was much more at ease than when we entered. I suggested we take a cab to Forty-fifth Street and show Jack "our" theatre. He liked the idea, but wanted to walk. A warm night—the first this year. Broadway teeming. Jack pointed out various theatres he'd played in. We turned down Forty-fifth Street. Jack was impressed that the theatre beside ours houses Alec Guinness in *Dylan*. Across the street is *Oliver*, on the other side of us is *Beyond the Fringe*. Ed, Ulu, Jack and I regarded "our" marquee. Ulu left us to meet Irene. Ed, Jack and I had a drink at Downey's. Jack seemed to be getting his "sea legs."

April 20

First reading at noon today. Edgar gave a cocktail party for the company at his home yesterday afternoon. Ruth and I arrived a bit after five. Blanche was there, Paul Leaf, Jules Fisher (who will probably do the lighting), Joe Beruh and his wife Kathleen Murray and their son, Max Eisen, Fred and Rose Morgan (backers who live in Ed's building—he owns the *Hudson Review*), Martin and Janet Sheen and one of their children, Rose and Ulu, Jack and Irene. Neither Martin nor Irene had ever met Jack before. They seemed to get on nicely. They looked like a "real," as opposed to a "stage," family. The atmosphere was subdued, congenial and optimistic. Jack begins to unwind—finding this fresh audience for a lot of old gags he'd never dare tell in Hollywood helps. Everyone likes him. It has taken a lot of courage for him to come here, and we are aware of it. He told us amusing things about his work as straight man with Bert Lahr, whom he mimicked beautifully. Two of the people who had pledged me $1,000 apiece will not be able to fulfill their pledge. I called Dave Fink and Dan Featherston (classmates at Dartmouth) for dough. Dan said to send him the forms and he'd see what he could do with some people he knows. I leave for the first reading in a few minutes. Ruth just came to me and wept for joy at her delight that this day is finally come. I have a sore throat, and it's raining, but I feel a quiet confidence at the center of me.

April 21

Got to the city at eleven-thirty. Checked the car at the Fifty-seventh Street place on a monthly basis. Took a cab to 524 West Fifty-first Street (Tait's Warehouse), between Tenth and Eleventh avenues. It is a rectangular cinder-block building. We use the second floor: a perfect setup for a floating crap game. The floor is taped to the dimensions of the Royale stage—dummy props are set up. It's a clean place. Hot-air heat. Very hot or very cold all day. Paul Leaf, George Blanchard and Martin were there before me. The others arrived pretty much on time. Edgar was there a bit later, stayed a short while, came back later for another spell. Joe Beruh was in late in the day. Ulu sat at one end of the table. Irene at his left, Martin across, Jack at Ulu's right. I sat next to Ulu, a bit away from the table. Ulu explained that he wanted nothing forced in the first reading—or in the initial stages of rehearsal. He said that if they started to play before they really understood, it would waste time, because those bad habits would have to be broken before the right way could be pursued. He said he wanted to find out what they didn't feel or understand at this point, rather than what they did. That relaxed everyone a bit—took some of the pressure off. He asked the actors to look at each other—to maintain visual contact, even though it might mean fumbling as their eyes sought the next line of the script. Irene and Martin did this readily.

For Jack it was difficult. He is extremely shy—admitted it later, as Ulu began to open him up. The first reading took three hours. This included a couple of breaks between scenes. It was to me, overall, most encouraging. I felt my intuition about Jack was a sound one. Martin has a nervous smile and laugh that will have to be reined in. Jack will have trouble opening to Martin in their "love" scene, and he fell off a bit in the climax of Act One. Was not aggressive enough with Irene. Irene will have to avoid anger at a few points. But the overall indications were *excellent*. We all went to lunch feeling fine. Jack, Ulu, Paul and I ate in a place on Eleventh Avenue (Clara's). Irene went off alone, as did Martin. I could tell that Jack was much relieved. His jokes kept things happy all day. At one point he and Irene did a Pat Rooney dance. They seem to get on nicely. Jack respects both her and Martin. They are all workers. When Ulu asks Jack a personal question, he gets a joke response, at which he laughs genuinely—and then, the joke having broken the barrier, pursues his question to deeper ground. Jack squirms at this but co-operates as best he can. For example: at the point where John Cleary tells of meeting Nettie, Ulu stopped the reading and asked Jack how he met his own wife. Jack, with no pause, said, "I just opened my wallet and there she was." We all laughed and then Ulu, gently but firmly, prodded Jack to the true recital. After the first reading, Ulu gave his interpretation of the play—invited questions—then started a second reading, stopping for any question or at any point where he felt the subtext required explanation. I occasionally volunteered a point, or was asked to clarify a motivation. By eight o'clock, we were only through Act One in this fashion. Ulu said—and all agreed—it was a fine day's work. Paul Leaf was most enthused—felt the script was like a piece of chamber music. Jack and I walked five blocks in the rain before we got a cab. My throat very sore last night. Arrived home at 10:00 P.M.

April 22

Arrived at Tait's at noon yesterday. The overall rehearsal was in most ways a letdown after the first day. It will be very tough to unlock Jack. Ulu tried having him and Martin chat—but Jack parried all attempts to get personal. This will work beautifully for us if we can, at the climactic moment, have him open up. At the end of the day, Ulu confided that he now realized he would have to handle Jack differently—that what Jack needs is confidence. Irene was consistently excellent—and experiments with points she is already master of. Martin gradually understanding. The more he understands the less we see that nervous smile. We have much work to do—but the indications hold at favorable. We all ate at that luncheonette. The owner gave Jack a free package of Tums as we exited. Dave Fink called; he's putting in $200. Dan Featherston called; he's good for $800 at least.

April 23

Rain again. Got to the warehouse at noon. Nothing much was happening as they read. Ulu stopped them—had Jack improvise the opening scene on stage with Irene. Jack was most uncomfortable. Pulled his head in like a turtle. Irene was actually abusing him, and he was taking it passively. Completely wrong—the character I wrote would not have stood for it. Ulu stopped them, reminded Jack that the mother tells the son that she's always been afraid of the father. Jack and Irene did the improvisation again. Still Jack did not react to her abuse. If Ulu had told him directly to act angry, he would have done it, and credibly, but the ultimate thing, the pinnacle moment, can only happen if that anger (and everything else) is born within Jack, and not imposed from the outside. Working as a second banana all these years seems to have sapped some of Jack's capacity for indignation. Our problem is to make a top banana out of a second banana. We went to lunch feeling a bit down. How would we open Jack up? Could we? Ulu accomplished the transition so smoothly that it wasn't till the afternoon that I fully realized we had graduated from the table to the stage. The set in outline seems most comfortable. The blocking seems natural. Jack and Martin were doing the second scene of Act One—were at the point where Jack is telling Martin how he met the mother. Nothing was happening. Ulu stopped them. Told Jack to take a lot of time. "I don't care if you take three minutes between lines," he said. In short, he wanted Jack to try and visualize—to make the words real to himself. He also took Jack aside for a brief chat. The scene resumed. Jack was speaking of the blue dress the mother wore, and suddenly it was real to him. HOW DELIGHTED WE ALL WERE! Ulu complimented him. That opening-up gave Jack a real lift. He began to show much more authority. I think it was a major breakthrough. Martin was playing (dully) a scene with Irene. Ulu took *him* aside. I don't know what transpires in these little talks, but Martin came back galvanized. Played a fierce bit with Irene. It was actually too much—but it was wonderful to see all the stops out for the first time. Wonderful to know that capacity was there. We all felt good at the end of the day. Joe Beruh dropped Jack and Paul and Martin off, then drove Ulu and me to Max's for a meeting with himself and Ed. We agreed on the artwork. Decided on flyers, posters and a teaser campaign. They want me to do a Sunday piece. But on what? Our set is being built in New Jersey for $4,000. I met Alvin Cooperman briefly. We'd met once before at the Country Mart in Brentwood, when we both lived in Los Angeles. Ed and I had a sandwich at Sardi's—congratulated ourselves on ever getting this far. I arrived home at 1:00 A.M.

April 24

Arrived at rehearsal a little after noon. Bert Andrews is our photographer. It's his first Broadway show. He took some pictures of me (having already done the others) and left. Ulu spent the day blocking the first scene, which is a quarter of the script, and the most difficult *to* block. It was slow, tedious work setting all that movement. When the scene was run through, it was still rough and awkward, but I did feel the arc of it—was pleased. Ulu uses the stage well. Jack still lost in the opening bit of Scene One. He clings to anything that will permit him not to look into Irene's eyes. How to make him aggressive is the key problem at present. Jack's portraits taken yesterday are worthless because he did a comic take in most of them and glared dourly in the others. We'll have new pictures taken today. Rehearsal starts at eleven today.

April 25

Ulu blocked the second scene of Act One. Nice things taking rough shape. Jack not feeling well. We made an appointment to see a Dr. Baldwin on Sixty-eighth Street at five forty-five. At two we broke for lunch. Ulu, Paul and I went shopping for a dance record, looked at a kitchen table, ate lunch. Came back to Tait's. Ed was there—furious because his name in the Funke story is printed as "Frank" Lansbury, and Ulu's last name has an extra *s*. Also, we didn't get the lead position after keeping the story exclusive for Funke, at his request, for all this time. Bert Andrews came at five and retook Jack's portraits. Jack was resistant —wanted make-up, which I talked him out of. I felt his fatigue and no make-up would work for us—added character to his face. I took him by cab to the doctor. He had a fever. The doctor gave him penicillin, and a pre-

66

scription which I had filled while he got some things at the Osborne so he could stay overnight at my house. A nice drive up here. He was shivering when we arrived—but still telling jokes. He ate well. I gave him a Seconal and he went to bed at ten forty-five. Oh yes, and despite his fever and condition he still played the piano and sang a few songs before retiring. Ulu called to say Jack didn't have to come in till twelve-thirty today. Ed called. He and Joe Beruh had gone over our budget and found us in good shape.

April 26

Jack was still wobbly when he awoke yesterday. We had breakfast before he rose. Waffles! And the first batch stuck! I left it to Jack whether he felt well enough to rehearse. He postponed decision till after he ate—finally decided to go in and do as much as he felt up to. He embraced Ruth affectionately. I'm sure he appreciated the solicitude that was directed at him. We had a good talk while driving in. He wondered why he had never become a star, when he always knew, within himself, that he was more talented than most of the fellows he played second to. I reminded him of his remark the night before about his never wanting the responsibility inherent in a marriage. I suggested that the same avoidance of responsibility might have blocked his career: it's only the top banana who takes the rap when a show fails. He was much improved at rehearsal—so much more in command that Ulu and I both suggested he try to run a fever every day. Dave Fink, who was passing through town, was at the warehouse when Jack and I arrived. Ulu said it was all right for Dave to observe from the side. Dave was instantly engaged by what was happening, though he'd never read the script. This was encouraging to me, for I've always contended that if a thing is truly alive your interest will be engaged no matter where you happen to dip in. Irene, Jack, Martin, Paul, Ulu, Dave and

I went to the restaurant in that motel on Tenth Avenue.
A nice lively lunch—spiced by the shared feeling of a good
morning's work. Dave insisted on treating us all. After
lunch he saw a bit more and left. I was prepared to go
home early, but Jack seemed most desirous for my company
at dinner. I could feel his loneliness. I called Ruth, who
said I should go with him by all means. Ulu is wonderful
about taking suggestions, which reveals a true self-confi-
dence. Jack has the choice, by contract, of dressing rooms.
Told there was only one "star's" room downstairs, he said
he thought he'd offer it to Irene. I said that I was sure it
would be appreciated. I can't see beyond the opening. I am
exhausted, but I want the rehearsals to never end.

April 27

Rehearsal started at eleven o'clock yesterday. I arrived
after twelve. They broke for lunch at two. We went to
that motor court place again. Coming back from lunch we
observed the transom to the warehouse roof open, which
meant that the man who keeps pigeons up there was tend-
ing his birds. Jack climbed the iron ladder, stuck his head
out, and asked the man if there were any messages. I left at
five-fifteen. Ulu told me that Jack had misconstrued his
(Ulu's) laughter the day before as a criticism instead of a
genuine appreciation. Ulu reassured him. Called Ulu when
I got home to say how good I felt—and how pleased I am
with his work.

April 28

I kept a morning appointment with a television producer in from Hollywood. He'd seen the *New York Times*
item about *Roses*. He asked about our budget. When he
learned how small it was, and that we had no stars, his
interest in the project vanished. He said the proper things
(good luck, etc.), but I knew that he had no sense of my
feelings, no awareness of the thrill it is to do something for

Author Frank Gilroy and Director Ulu Grosbard in discussion during rehearsals of *The Subject Was Roses*

love. About yesterday's rehearsal: Martin seemed physically depleted and emotionally depressed. It hurt his playing with Irene. Dave Fink called. He found an investor: Carroll Terrell, an English teacher at the University of Maine. Dave told him of *Roses* and he volunteered $1,000. I called Terrell and confirmed this. Am sending him the forms this morning. I told the cast. Since Dave was the first thing remotely resembling an audience that we'd had, it gave us all a lift to have him go away with such enthusiasm. The rest of the day went well. Martin got better. Jack was much improved all day. Irene was even.

April 29

Ruth's great quote as I left yesterday for an interview at Sardi's: "Remember—one drink, confident but modest, and don't knock anybody." Rained all day. Martin seems depressed. His wife and children have gone to visit her family in Ohio. Jack was excellent all day. Really opening up. Ulu improvised Jack and Martin in Scene 2, Act Two. It got pretty violent. Martin's anger came out. I left for the luncheon interview at Sardi's not encouraged by the morning's work, but aware that Martin's mood is transitory. After the interview, I ran over to the Royale, in the rain, arriving just as the placards about our show were delivered. It was not the jolt I expected. Seemed natural, as though I'd been through it before. I suspect the first view of the marquee when it's decorated will be different. Back to rehearsal: Martin still not right but improved. Irene and Jack superb. We saw two beautiful sequences. Everyone felt a surge of joy and accomplishment. How fine this *could* be! I had a sandwich with Ulu and Martin and came home. A most encouraging day.

April 30

The days are blurring . . . Some good moments yesterday, especially for Irene. I can feel various parts of the play taking definite shape. Jack flies to the Coast tonight to complete his part in the movie *How To Murder Your Wife*. We had him call the director to make sure they would shoot his scene tomorrow and not hang him up till Monday. Jack is entirely with us in this, doesn't want to miss any rehearsals, which is a good sign. You sit for hours sometimes, and all the dialogue is lifeless. You blame your own fatigue, or the actors', or both. You begin to blame the script. The whole project seems stillborn. You are so depressed—and then suddenly, before you know it, your attention is entirely on the playing area. Life is going on there. The miracle is happening. And no movie footage can ever duplicate that experience. Joe Beruh brought our flyers in. They're all in red—and most attractive. Gave everyone a lift.

May 1, 1964

Then to rehearsal. Stuart Little of the *Herald Tribune* was waiting for me with Max Eisen. He had interviewed me by phone the day after *Plowboy* opened. Max, Little, Edgar and I went to the Motor Lodge for lunch. The interview was painless, smooth. He took almost no notes—seemed to enjoy himself. He got so caught up in the economy of our venture that he offered to pay for his own lunch. Back to rehearsal. Ruth and Pauline arrived. Ulu had no objection to their presence. Jack was all dressed and ready for his trip to the Coast. They had been rehearsing since 10:00 A.M. to get in a full day before he departed. Ruth felt the reality and ensemble spirit, and enjoyment of the players, even though they kept going over and over the same bits. On leaving, she let everyone know how good she felt about everything. Time neared for Jack's departure. Our posters had arrived. They looked handsome. We wrapped one for Jack to take home. They were doing the end of Scene 3, Act One—the part where Jack tries to make Irene. Feeling good about everything, Jack played this section with unprecedented vigor. As the full strength of what I'd written came to life, I was jolted. When I thought of how glibly I'd been saying the play was "highly autobiographical" I winced. What will people who liked my parents think? YIKES! Ulu had, for other reasons, told me to mute the autobiography confession. He, sympathizing with my shock (and pleased that he had brought the scene to such fruition), counseled me to "cool" all talk of autobiography from now on. I certainly shall. Now Jack was to depart. Everyone bid him a most fond and affectionate farewell. He could not mistake the sincerity of what was said. Irene gave him a St. Christopher's medal, which touched him deeply. As I put him in a cab, I said, "You were worth waiting for." He was a foot taller leaving town than when he arrived. Who the hell cares if the play makes money—these are the days, the moments, that redeem life. Joe Beruh drove me to a radio interview. When we were off the air Joe said, "I'll bet that didn't sell two tickets," implying that the interviewer had not done his job properly. It was an uncalled-for remark. I apologized for Joe —who then tried to apologize for himself. The interviewer would not shake hands with him. I left Joe at Eighth Avenue and Forty-fifth Street, walked past MY theatre—the posters are up but nothing else. I felt somewhat out of control; went to a movie. Saw half of *Silence*. It did not have nearly the impact of *Through a Glass Darkly*. Of course, I'm in no frame of mind to judge anything unrelated to *Roses*.

May 2

Dictated some twenty letters—enclosed *Roses* circulars and asked people to help us get business during preview week. Many more letters to do. Ruth is getting into the spirit of it now—sold six tickets herself at the drugstore this morning. Arrived at rehearsal at about 1:30 P.M. I was told the marquee was up. I called Jim McLaughlin and met him in front of the Royale. The sign looks beautiful. I did not get the charge I would have ten years ago, but still it was very nice. Actually it looked natural. I've worked that hard, that I feel I deserve it. Jim and I had a couple of drinks. He came back to meet the actors at the warehouse, but I eased him out when they started to work. It didn't seem an opportune moment for visitors. Martin was having a bad day. His confidence and his energy seemed down. I think Jack's going affected him. I think he'll be all right ultimately. Ulu worked with Martin till eleven Thursday night, and stayed late again last night. Ulu feels the dancing, which is so hard for Martin, is sapping his confidence. He's getting better at it, but you don't learn to dance confidently in a week. Martin is such a willing worker: all that effort can accomplish will be done. Irene has a groove. She fluctuates within it. Her dedication is frightening—a religion, really. Jack called from the Coast at 11:00 P.M. our time to say he was getting a plane at eleven their time. He sounded joyous and anxious to return. I felt he was checking to see if we were really here, and not something he dreamed. Stuart Little's interview appeared in the *Tribune* yesterday. An excellent article. Caught the flavor exactly. His quotes were right on the nose, and he'd hardly taken a note. Jim Mathews, a free-lance photographer, started shooting the rehearsals. My contact with the world is restricted to news broadcasts on the car radio. Our marquee is prettier than *Dylan's*.

May 3

Got to rehearsal a bit after noon yesterday. Paul Leaf's thirty-fifth birthday. Martin generally improved yesterday. Jack arrived at two. All welcomed him warmly, and vice versa. The family was back together. We lunched at the motor court. Irene surprised Paul with a birthday cake and candles, which he extinguished at a blow. Jack worked excellently. Ulu seemed to break into fresh grounds of understanding with Martin and Irene in the end of Scene 1, Act Two. Will try to solidify it today. Irene did the next-to-last scene. It's good now—but could be *magnifico* by opening night. Ulu and Jack and I went to see the marquee (which they had not seen before) after rehearsal. We were all delighted with ourselves. Jack, clenched fists raised to heaven, vowed, "Forty-fifth Street, I'll lick you yet." We dined at Downey's. Jack had a complaint—too much talk between Ulu and me when they are doing scenes. This is largely my fault, and I said so and told him it would cease. Jack brought his golf clubs back from the Coast. How bullish can you get?

May 5

Felt a breakthrough with Martin late Sunday afternoon. He'd been playing poorly all day. Ulu kept talking to him and then the light dawned: "They're like babies," Martin said, referring to the parents. "I know more than they do." With this new awareness, he played a scene very much improved. I drove him and Jack home here for dinner. After Ruth's rigatoni, we sat around the piano with Jack playing and singing and us joining in when we knew the lyrics, till after midnight. It felt good to relax. After breakfast yesterday morning, Jack and Martin hit a few golf balls around while I got the car ready. One of Martin's shots struck Jack—no damage, thank God. During the ride to the city, Jack and Martin ran lines. I dropped them at the parking lot. Stopped at Blanche's briefly—made a bank deposit for Martin so that he wouldn't be late for rehearsal. How bright and splendid Fifth Avenue and everyone on it looked. I could make a case for the most unpleasant face. Took a cab to the Royale—gave the cabbie one of our flyers.

We had rented the theatre (for $50) just for the day. It is impossible to get any perspective on what you're doing in the warehouse. When I arrived at the Royale I found a reporter from *The New Yorker* waiting for me with Max and Ed. He is one of the people who write the "Talk of the Town." We took him to lunch at Sardi's. As expected, a *New Yorker* interview is different. Where other interviewers ask questions, this fellow sat in silence—waited for me to hang myself. He's "New Yorker" Irish but I found myself liking him. He came back to the theatre with us and sat awhile. I don't know what he took away. Being in the theatre for the first time really shook everyone up. No one could remember lines, etc. Martin, under the pressure of the place, went back to a concept of the part he had discarded days ago. Jack began to exaggerate. Irene did her big scene superbly. Just sitting alone on the stage in an old bathrobe, while the others were conferring at one side, she commanded your attention and feeling. Ulu had another long session with Martin, they played Scene 2, Act Two again and it showed life. On that note the day ended at 8:00 P.M. Since being there was such a trauma, we are going to take the theatre again, probably next Monday. Edgar says we have thirty-one or thirty-two grand, not counting the four he and I put up for Equity bonds. There is more to write—but no time.

May 6

A quickie; rehearsal starts at nine today, because they're going out to Lambertville to see the set. Jack showed surprising and very real emotion in the last scene yesterday. If he can hold back his tears for another few lines, it will be perfect. Martin is better. Thinking of cutting the joke and the handkerchief bit. False, I feel. Must watch the script now. They're adding a lot of handles which deprive the play of precision. I spoke at Sardi's to Blanche's

Woman Pays Club. Linda Gaydos (Ruth's niece) joins us tomorrow—will be Ulu's script girl, etc. My mind is on tightening the script.

May 7

I was in a sullen mood when I left the house yesterday morning. When I arrived at rehearsal, my irritation crystallized. I found myself regarding the play and players with a cold, clinical eye. They were in the midst of a scene. I followed the play text and found a word added or omitted in every other speech. I let Ulu know of my dissatisfaction. Paul and I had been telling him how far off the lines they were, but it never seemed to register. Now I really underlined the point. Ulu told Paul to stop them every time they erred from now on. Paul did this. The consequence: they made so many mistakes that they couldn't play a scene. Ulu was shocked and said I should have told him earlier. I said I hadn't wanted to intrude on the development of a feeling for the play, and was hoping he'd catch them himself. My mood now carried over to other areas. I felt we were being seduced by the happy aura of our little group. I stepped outside the circle and watched. I cut out the joke and the handkerchief bits, with Ulu's concurrence. I also suggested that a lot of that vaudeville business was overdone. Ulu experimented at muting it and the results were excellent. Martin played his "turning on Irene" scene excellently. He never raised his voice, and was stunned at the results he achieved with words alone. He couldn't contain his delight. Ulu had been telling him this for two weeks, but now the truth really hit him. It was like watching the sun come up. Don Foote, the costumer, came over to measure. I insisted Irene use her own hat. I love that hat.

May 8

Rehearsal began at noon yesterday. It was not distin-

guished. Still the same trouble over lines. I emphasized my
concern. Ulu and I went to the Actors Studio during the
lunch break so we could post the *Roses* flyers. Met Shelley
Winters there. She told me how much she liked the play—
said she turned it down because she didn't want to play the
mother of a twenty-one-year-old boy. Ulu was uncertain
about having a run-through in the afternoon. I urged him
to do so—felt we should do that once before inviting outsiders, as we plan to do today. He finally agreed. Joe Beruh
and Ed came over to the warehouse and filled me in on the
working details of box office operations: what protection
and jurisdiction we had, etc. Joe assured us there was no
flim-flam in a Shubert house—that every ticket was triple-
checked. They left. The stage was set for the run-through.
Linda, Paul, Ulu and I were the audience. Jim Mathews
was there to take pictures. The tension built amazingly.
The show began—our very first attempt to make a whole of
it. Jack did quite well in the first act and part of the
second act, fell apart in the last scene. Called for lines
again, and again. But he *was* in character. Irene was disappointing, but in character. Martin was disappointing
and *wasn't* in character—went back to that angry young
man that makes Timmy so unlikable and drains the play
of love. Numerous specific criticisms beyond this: the
peanuts; the touch; the vaudeville, etc. As the final "curtain" came down there was a great flood of relief on both
sides of the footlights. We and the players embraced like
old friends after a long separation. Ulu and I went aside.
He did not share my worry about Martin—felt more concerned for Jack. He also wants more time to work those
peanuts in. It was not a disaster, but we're a long, long
way from home. Today we'll run at five for a few
guests. Good. The more pressure the better at this point.
Home at nine-thirty. Tired and a bit down. But I still feel

at bottom that we'll win—only we must win *big*, and that means perfection.

May 9

Ruth brought out my summer suits. I put on a light gray flannel that I'd forgotten about. It looked fine and gave me just the proper lift to begin the day. It was wise to look bright and chipper for the cast after the first run-through. I arrived at the rehearsal hall at ten-thirty. The cast arrived—went over the opening scene. Jack doesn't seem to grasp that initial mood. I felt myself getting stale and querulous, so I left. Had a drink and sandwich at Whyte's. Got a haircut. Walked down Fifth Avenue (85°) to Fifty-first Street, no cabs available. Over to Broadway, where I stopped for a soda. At five we had the first run-through for "outsiders"—Rose, Blanche, George Morrison, Edgar, Ruth, and the regulars, Linda, Paul, etc. The overall effect was much improved over the day before. We all came away feeling we had much work to do, but optimistic. Martin was fine in Act One, but went back to the angry young man in Scenes 1 and 2 of Act Two. Edgar, in his criticism afterward, went right to that as his main complaint. A lot of lines blown, and several stops. But overall, there was a bullish feel. The tendency now is to want to sit a moment and rest, but that is wrong. NOW is the time to press, to pursue the advantage to the limits of our energy. And so it's back to work at 11:00 A.M. We're getting some preview ticket orders. All departments seem in control. Blanche invited us to her place after the run-through. This is a good indication of a favorable response from her. Rose Gregorio (after Act One) whispered to me, "Why don't you write a part for me in your next play?" Jack took Rose, Ruth and Blanche to Blanche's. Ed drove me. George and Ulu stopped for a private drink—director talk. Ruth and I arrived home around ten. Exhausted, but with visions of sugar plums.

May 10

Rehearsal began at eleven yesterday. I gave Ulu my detailed notes on the previous day's run-through—told him again that my overall feel, and Ruth's, was most optimistic. He said Rose felt the same. Ulu worked and worked on the second scene of Act Two. Martin did not improve. Ulu tried improvisations and physical activities and everything he could think of to break the grip of what is hampering Martin. No success. Martin is aware of the problem and trying so hard. Maybe *too* hard. Jack hates the picture of himself at the Royale—insists it come down. Ulu and I are in tune on what needs to be done.

May 11

I was outside the warehouse at ten-forty yesterday. I was the first arrival—sat in my car. I enjoy the vibrancy and variety of that neighborhood. Too bad they can't renovate such areas without sterilizing them. Irene arrived—sat in the car with me. Then Martin joined us. Then Jack came. And then Ulu, with the key. Everyone had a let's-get-to-work air. Ulu spent almost all day on the first act. You could feel the improvement as things were polished and firmed. First scene—the first few minutes, especially—need work still. Just before we broke at night, Ulu had Martin try that second scene in Act Two. They had cooked up, between them, a way to try and break the impasse. It consisted of Martin playing in a Jimmy Stewart voice. Jack, who knew nothing in advance, reacted beautifully. Suddenly there was life onstage. Now they did the scene straight and tried to achieve the same effect—succeeded sufficiently to make us feel that a real breakthrough had been achieved. AN EXCELLENT DAY'S WORK! We're hiring Matt Clark and Joe Sullivan as understudies. Matt will double as assistant stage manager. Learned the Shuberts will charge us $80 per show for air conditioning. I gather this is usual, but we have no provision for it in our budget, which hurts. Why do they charge for the cold, when they don't charge for the hot? Jack told Paul to offer Irene the first dressing room. Jack gets better each day. Max brought the preview program over for approval. He urges me to do a Sunday newspaper piece. I resist. I've always hated those before-the-fact things. I'm moving into the Fifth Avenue Hotel today, because we begin twelve-hour rehearsals.

May 12

Checked in at the hotel. Went to Bob Ehrenbard's to drop off the agreement—he's putting $300 more, at his own insistence, into *Roses*. Says he detects a miracle in the making. Went to the Royale. Met Joc Bcruh. Twenty-three more pieces of mail, all preview stuff, came in. The box office is open. My feeling is that we'll do better during preview week than is anticipated. Joe figures four or five grand. I say eight or nine and secretly expect ten. Spent a few minutes at Max's office. You could feel the tempo picking up. To Sardi's and an interview with Len Harris of the *World-Telegram*. Joe and Ed arrived, we went upstairs to Max's. I ordered $105-worth of opening-night tickets. I saw the opening-night chart. Over 150 seats reserved (free) for press, radio and television. Columbia Pictures called to buy two preview seats. I stole another look at the marquee. To the warehouse at 4:00 P.M. Rehearsal till seven. Martin was back to his old way in Act Two, Scene 2. Dinner break till eight o'clock. Linda ate with Paul, Ulu and me at a French place. Didn't like it. Was anyone else aware of a rather pugnacious guy at a nearby table who took exception to Ulu's lack of a haircut? He kept looking over with growing irritation. Long antenna are a burden. Run-through at eight. We can be 25 percent better—but last night was certainly a credit. Act One still seems dead for the first few minutes. Perhaps the audience's initial interest will cover that if we can't. Reaction was most encouraging. Our money situation as of yesterday: Capitalization, $40,000; money in, $33,600; Lansbury and Gilroy loan, $4,000; Lansbury balance, $2,400. Assuming we get reviews worth publicizing, the Blaine Thompson advertising company has given a written estimate that it will cost $19,897.60 to saturate papers and radio. Of course we don't have a dime in reserve for this—but I'm sure that if reviews are excellent, something will turn up.

May 13

Ulu came by the hotel at eight-thirty yesterday morning. We breakfasted. Then took a cab to Forty-sixth Street, where we met Don Foote and selected the material for Irene's dress in Act One. We went for a brighter hue since it is the point in the story when her hopes are highest. Ulu had another appointment. I walked over to Broadway. It was the first time I'd been on that street in the morning for many years. I had a cup of coffee in a place at Forty-fifth that enabled me to see down "our" street. I felt good. I was early for my ten-thirty meeting with Joe Beruh at the box office, strolled about peering into ticket brokers' to see where our poster was positioned. I forgot to say yesterday that on Monday night I'd dreamed that some supreme authority had forbidden us to use the rose with an eye as our logo. We could not open without it and all appeal was futile. Back to yesterday: I arrived at the Royale; met Leonard Cobb, who is the house treasurer. He invited me into the box office. I liked the sight of all those tickets in their various stalls. While he and I talked, an old woman came up to buy a preview ticket for an evening performance. She thought it would be $1.95 instead of the $2.50 that it was. For luck, I paid the difference. Ten pieces of mail yesterday. I don't know what happened over the counter. I went to Tait's. Rehearsal began at eleven. Martin and Irene worked very well. Made big gains. Ulu added some fine touches and cinched previous ones. I did notice Martin playing innocence in place of understanding in Act Two, Scene 1. Jack's performance is the most consistent. When he gets a good thing, he doesn't lose it. Lunch at two-thirty. Ulu, Irene, Jack and I went to the Motor Lodge. I took the afternoon off from four o'clock on. Came here to the hotel, watched most of an old "Thin Man" movie. Left at seven. Grabbed a hamburger. To the Royale. Ulu didn't want anyone but ourselves present at this runthrough. I'd called Ruth earlier. She said our cash is low. I told her I'd get back one of the two grand I loaned the company. I did this after explaining my situation to Ed. Ulu's brother Jack put in $1,600. Ruth's warning about our finances makes me realize that this is more of a gamble for me than the others suspect. I sat in the balcony for the first act. Martin could not project his likableness. He was "acting"—forcing. Jack was a rock. Irene was off: too private. I am being harsh, of course, since we had nothing but bare stage, and not a single prop—but now is the time to be harsh. Ulu sat in the balcony with me during the second act. He shares my criticism. I can't tell the actors they did well when I think they didn't. I feel it confuses them—ultimately makes them not trust you. To Downey's after. We were all exhausted. I'm glad we're off tomorrow. I think everyone needs a break. I still feel most confident—but I do wish Martin would exhibit a little consistency. Right now each performance is like a round of Russian roulette. Ulu and I dropped Irene off, then he dropped me.

May 14

Breakfasted at the hotel yesterday morning. The *Times* ad quoted Emory Lewis in *Cue* on *Plowboy*: "Gilroy reminds me of Odets and Chekhov, etc." I'm pleased by that, but I don't take it seriously. It isn't modesty that prevents me from doing so, but rather a strong sense of self-preservation. To Max's office to drop the Playbill biog off. Max is going to paper the first preview audience with off-Broadway casts who are off on Monday. Everyone says they're a generous audience, and could be good for word-of-mouth. Not much mail came in. The business we anticipated at the box office from running our ad on a matinee day did not materialize. We are canceling the Friday ad, and running a larger one on Monday. To the warehouse. Ulu spent a lot of time giving notes individually. Broke at two forty-five for lunch and a picture session at Bert Andrews' studio. I escorted Jack up to the Osborne to get his biography. We had a quick bite while he rewrote it. We all met at Bert Andrews'. Edgar and I saw that all was under control and departed. As we left, Bert said, "It's great to be connected with a hit," and I felt he meant it. Edgar and I went to Max's. I typed Jack's biography. Could any playwright do more? They told me that kids from my high school (DeWitt Clinton) wanted to interview me today. We set it for five-thirty at Max's. Ed and I told Joe that we wanted him to drop that characteristic pessimism. When people ask how tickets are going, he's been saying "Slow." We asked him to say "Surprisingly well." That's the spirit of this company and it should carry to every area, for it's a contagious thing. To the rehearsal hall. I felt exhausted. Martin was still playing innocence for understanding and had lost his vitality. I left. Went to the hotel—tried unsuccessfully to doze. Had supper and returned to Tait's. Had a nice chat with the cab driver. We became so engrossed that we were several blocks beyond my destination before I realized it. He killed the clock at once. I gave him a flyer, invited him to a dress rehearsal. Joe Sullivan, Jules Fisher, Tootsie Finkelstein (the prop man), Joe Beruh and Edgar were present for the run-through. It went so well that we applauded. I tore up my notes—told Martin I felt the character was his now, and that he should have fun with it. Irene and Jack were fine. Jack is getting better and better and better. Fisher anticipates no problem with the lights. The timing for this day off couldn't be better. We still have much work to do. The big problem: can we transfer our fragile intimate warehouse production to the Royale without losing it?

May 15

Ruth and I made a list for the after-opening party. It comes to 25 so far. She drove into the city with me at four o'clock. Heavy rain. Left my bags at Blanche's. Went to Max's office to meet the DeWitt Clinton boys. I felt bad because we were a bit late, and arrived to learn they could not make it. Advance ticket sales are poor. I still feel we'll do well during previews. It will be a last-minute business. We went to the theatre, where the set was up and Jules Fisher was in the process of lighting. The set is excellent —exudes a previous life. Ed put a door between the rooms. Ulu and I don't like it, but we'll try it a bit before making a decision. Jules radiates skill and efficiency. The glimpse of certain effects was beautiful. Joe Beruh drove Ruth and me to the Morgans' cocktail party. Their apartment is the same as Ed's, but lower in the building. The place was swarming when we arrived. The *Hudson Review* was the centerpole. I heard Alberto Moravia was present, but never encountered him—never made it to the living room. Joan and Bill Clifford were there. Philip and Margret Booth were introduced to us. He's a poet whose father taught me (English 19) at Dartmouth. John Simon (of the *Hudson Review*) was introduced to me. I thanked him for his words about *Plowboy*. We both (perhaps it was only me) felt the awkwardness of our situation—since he would be judging *Roses* in a week—and the conversation ended. He's the first critic of my work that I've ever met. I have this thing about writers and critics. Like baseball players and umpires—I feel they should not socialize. There was much talk of *Roses*. Jack arrived—and then Irene. There is an unmistakable condescension on the part of the literati toward the theatre—and though I resent it, I must say that the theatre, as a whole, has done little to warrant anyone's respect or attention. Ruth and I and Jack and Ed went back to the theatre to watch a bit more of the lighting process. Rose and Ulu met us there. We all went to Downey's to eat. Ruth left for home at eleven. I picked up my bags at Blanche's and came back to the theatre. Jules completed the lighting at midnight. Joe Beruh drove Ulu and me home. Everything is set up—and ahead of schedule.

May 16

To the Royale at 11:00 A.M. Ulu was there. Jules Fisher was setting lights. Ulu and I went to the warehouse. The cast was there at noon. Rehearsal till two-thirty. The final hour was spent with us all around a table and reading the script—which is exactly how we began four weeks ago. While they read, Matt cleaned up what had been the playing area. Though he is understudying Martin, you feel that he really wants Martin to succeed—helps him in every way possible. I'm sure that's unusual. We left Tait's for the last time. Thanked Irving for his generous treatment. As Paul Leaf predicted, I had grown fond of that place. Jack, Irene, Martin, Linda and I took a cab to the theatre, dropped our gear, then went to Downey's for lunch. A curious thing: Irene will not ever view the set from out front—feels that it threatens her sense of reality about the play. At Downey's, three boys from DeWitt Clinton (Pete, Jim and Art) came to photograph and interview me. I sat in a booth with them. I resisted the urge to pontificate, refused to make any general statement on the "state of the theatre," etc. I took them to the theatre. I think our lack of stars, the unlit set, and the work-a-day atmosphere was disillusioning to them. One of the boys let something slip that indicated he was writing us off as a flop. The technical rehearsal was a long-drawn-out affair. Went on to midnight. Then a picture call. We finished at 1:00 A.M. We will be in ragged shape for tonight's dress rehearsal. I hear Frank Loesser might be there tonight as a potential investor. We're not telling Ulu or the others, so that they won't be disappointed if he doesn't come through. Frank Vasti (my uncle) and Fred and Rose Bachmann brought the sixteen-year-old daughter of a friend to interview me for her school paper. I invited them into the theatre—suggested her impressions might be the basis of an article. Frank and Fred were impressed by Jack's resemblance to my father. Ulu dropped me off here at the hotel at 1:30 A.M. I slept till eight-thirty this morning. I feel no anxiety about going before an audience. To be honest, I'm eager for it—like a well-trained fighter.

May 17

Went out to the Cookery for breakfast yesterday morning, but it wasn't open till eleven. A beautiful morning. I strolled through the Square. Met John Tobias (a writer friend) at the chess tables. He took me to the Rienzi for breakfast and a chess game. We got into the mechanics of writing—shop talk—and it was most refreshing for me. We were the only customers at that hour. I thought of Roger, and so many similar writer-to-writer talks years ago. John walked me back to the hotel. I invited him and Pat to the dress rehearsal. To the theatre at noon. The stage door man gave me a white rose and a nice note, both from Irene. There was much activity at the theatre all day. Props, painting, lights, costumes and even some rehearsing. Standing outside the theatre at one point, I was approached by a familiar face—Hank Heffernan, from my old neigh-

85

borhood in the Bronx. Hadn't seen him since 1951 when
we were both messengers at Young & Rubicam. He's an
actor now. I invited him to the dress rehearsal. Saw the
pictures taken the night before. One group shot—all three
actors laughing (genuinely) at a joke Jack's just told—is
excellent. It will be our program cover. Even Jack liked
it! Went out for bagels and lox, and a coffee ice cream
soda. Am I pregnant? Only forty seats sold so far for Monday night. Ulu, Jack, Paul, Joe and I went to Downey's for
supper at six-thirty. Met Jerry O'Laughlin (who played
the Plowboy), who said he would be at the dress rehearsal.
How did he know about it? I began to suspect we would
have more than the dozen or so people that I anticipated.
Back to the theatre. By eight o'clock the lobby was jammed.
To make a long one short, we had 400 people there. What
a shock! To go from five people in a warehouse to four
hundred in a theatre—and with no transition!! Well, they
did splendidly. They can do much better, but for a first
audience showing, it was an excellent indication. I sat with
Rose Gregorio in the last row at the right side. All the
laughs I expected (and that few believed were there) came
through—plus a couple we can do without. It was like that
first *Plowboy* preview, but not so extreme. Martin came
through the best. Jack blew lines. Martin helped him at
one point. But no one ever went out of character. Irene
was too soft-spoken—not projecting. I felt she didn't admit
the presence of the audience. Lots of lighting things went
off—naturally. Three curtain calls. At Jack's suggestion
they took company calls rather than individual ones. It prevents any threat to the ensemble feel that is so essential.
Blanche and the Tobiases were delighted, though aware of
the places that didn't work. No word on Loesser's reaction. I saw no one leave at intermission, or at any other
time. To Downey's with Ulu and Rose. Jack joined us.

George Morrison joined us. Called Ruth. To bed by 1:30 A.M.

May 18

To the theatre at noon yesterday. Irene somewhat resistant to direction, and quibbling about bits of business that warranted no attention. Ulu handled her well. We had a run-through at eight-thirty just for ourselves. They played low key but you could feel their swelling confidence. Saturday night's audience really served us well. Of course, they could have injured us just as strongly. Jack, after Act One, complained his good eye was bothering him. Ulu left it up to him to continue or not. He went on. Still many flaws in the play. I made a couple of changes, to kill laughs we didn't want. Joe says Zolotow in the *Times* is not giving us anything because we gave Funke (also on the *Times*) the first story. What kind of nonsense is that? And what happened to all the interviews I was to have? I called Edgar this morning and told him how displeased I was. Other irritations of the moment: that pitiful small ad in the *Times* on our first day before a paying audience. Also, Frank Squibb (a friend) called—never got the tickets he ordered a week ago, and Dave Fink called. His letter to the Royale came back marked "address unknown." I guess it's my day to vent my anxiety on petty details. I'll guard against it.

May 19

To the theatre at twelve-thirty yesterday. They spent the day going over light cues and entrances and exits. We're toning down the kitchen to get rid of that comedy, never-never-land feel. Changed the tablecloth, painted the chairs gray. Other lighting and paint changes are to be made. Jack had a hassle about his other suit: walked out of a fitting. They got it finished by last night, after a slight row. It seems that to get anything accomplished on time, one

must holler. Had a sandwich at the theatre. Edgar picked
me up at four. We went to Fernbach's and closed the
corporation. I had to invest one grand (the one I'd loaned
previously) and Ed invested $3,400 to complete the
$40,000. John Fernbach seemed amazed that we were
within our budget. We told John and Frank Weissburg and
Richard Bloomenthal that we felt things were going well.
Frank called a woman ("knowledgeable about theatre")
who'd been to the dress rehearsal on Saturday. He asked
her how she liked the play. She (unaware of our presence)
said she didn't think it was any good, and was sure it
wouldn't run. No one on the inside thinks we're going
to pull this off. I took a Fifth Avenue bus to the hotel. Ruth
and I met Ulu and Rose at Joe's on MacDougal. Small and
quiet and not crowded, and good food. Just right for the
occasion. A most pleasant meal. Ulu and I dropped the
girls at Ohrbach's to look at dresses (for opening night)
while we went on to the theatre. There was quite a crowd
building. Saw several of the boys who'd read for the
Timmy role. We must have had close to 600 people. Most
were on comps. Joe said we did about $400. I want to get
exact figures today. The performance: overall it went well
—but it *must* go better if we're to get the brass ring. Martin
was superb. Jack was very good, but had a tendency to
overplay. We must get back to the reality of the play in
Act One. Act Two went excellently. The stage never went
black after one scene—we still may use curtains. At the
word "kikes" we got a single hiss. And I understand someone told Linda that they didn't see why the business about
the Jews had to be included "since there is already so much
hate in the world." It is alarming to be so misunderstood.
Many tearful faces coming up the aisle after the play. I
suspect this play may appeal more to the public than to the
critics. There were objections to Jack's punching Martin;
to Irene's lack of volume; to the empty beer cans. As Gene

Wolsk said, "When you're talking of these petty things after a preview, you know you're in pretty good shape." Had a nice telegram from John Gay, and a call from Marty Donovan at 1:00 A.M. to see how it went. Ruth says the tension during the show almost made her ill. I'm all right as long as I don't sit. The Thompsons loved the play, as did the Tomans. Knowing my family as well as they did, it was something more to them than a play. I was somewhat apprehensive about their reaction. And glad that the love came through.

May 20

Ruth and I breakfasted here. She left for home shortly after nine. I went to the theatre at eleven forty-five. Ulu went over our criticisms. He worked all afternoon—mostly with Irene. Must abbreviate now—in a hurry. I met the McLaughlins and her parents for dinner at Sardi's. Stopped off at the florist on Shubert Alley to get some flowers for Irene. While there, I heard a man tell the florist how "very warm" the show at the Royale was. I introduced myself; he is Cliff Hall, an actor in *Here's Love*. We did $380 last night. A small house since we didn't paper. First act went the worst it's ever gone. So bad that I hid at intermission. The second act was *excellent*—the best it's gone. Irene's scene went beautifully. Great audience response and reaction afterward. Leonard Soloway was there—came to me with moist eyes and said the play was onstage just as he had always envisioned it. That was extremely generous of him. Jack Grosbard (Ulu's brother) was there and sincerely moved. George Petrie was overwhelmed. And all this with no first act at all! We've decided to try curtains between scenes. Too confusing the other way.

May 21

Interview with Allan Wallach of *Newsday* (a Long Island paper) at Dinty Moore's. The matinee showed some improvement. Ruth arrived at four-thirty. We met the Zagorias for supper at Moore's. Watched the mob waiting for Elizabeth Taylor to fetch Richard Burton at the *Hamlet* stage door. Last night's performance was a further improvement over the matinee. The Zagorias, who had seen the play on Tuesday night, saw it again last night, at my invitation, and were amazed at the difference. Like many people, they think of a play as a frozen item and have no awareness of the tremendous fluctuation and change from one performance to another. They said it was the first time they had ever seen a play twice, and found it a most educational experience. Business again around $300.

May 22
Haircut. To the Royale. The kitchen was repainted. The new table was cut down. Irene had busted the other table last night in the dance sequence. When it happened she and Martin carried on so well that the audience thought it was planned. Ulu and the cast worked downstairs in the lounge while the painter worked on the set. I had lunch with Ed, Max and Joe. To kill an hour I went to McGirr's and played pool with Matt Clark. I returned to the hotel—napped a bit—changed clothes. Supper at the Sea Fare—one drink and wine. To the theatre at eight-fifteen. We had our best show to date last night. Irene much improved. Jack a bit too broad. Martin was just a bit cute. But overall it was a good show. Best response we've had. Max says Alexander Cohen's press agent thinks we might have the sleeper of the year.

May 23
Last night's show was down from Thursday's. The first scene and half of the second did not play. I met Ulu at Sixth Avenue and Forty-seventh Street. We got tuxedos for Monday. Ruth fetched me at the theatre at 3:00 P.M. We had a bite—went to Altman's—bought gifts (all in-

scribed 5/25/64) for all the actors and other members of the company. To Sardi's at six o'clock. Dinner with Dan and Rya Featherston. We did $475 last night. We have a total of $2,000 so far this week. That is much below what I'd anticipated. Ed says we are coming in for something under thirty grand—and that we can run next week if we don't make a dime. I am not sanguine this morning. Ruth went home after the show. Ulu and I had a drink with Edgar and Rosie. Jack needed a pep pill last night. Says he can't sleep. The past three shows to open on Broadway have been panned. The next opening is ours.

May 24

Matinee yesterday was the worst show we've done. Jack's energy way down. Ulu took Jack out for a three-hour talk and supper after the matinee. Ruth and I came down here to the hotel. We had a drink at the sidewalk café downstairs, and then another, and dinner at Longchamps. Being alone together like that had a most calming effect on me. Arrived at the theatre. Jack seemed quite restored after his talk with Ulu. I gave Irene a new line to say at her first entrance: "It's a lovely day." It sets her mood. She loves it. Last night's performance was the best we've played all week. If we could do as well tomorrow night, THEY'D HAVE TO LIKE US! Eddie Turro came up to me after the play and cried in my arms—and just phoned this minute to say again how moved he was, and how much he loved the show. I am deeply affected by his reaction, for he knew our family better than anyone. Back to yesterday: I'd decided to go home to Monroe with Ruth after last night's show. I thought it might be good for Jack to come with me. Ulu agreed. I asked Jack before the show and he accepted. Jack made the second scene in Act One work as it never has before. Ruth and Jack and I had a drink with Rosie and Ed and Ulu after the show and drove home. Gave Jack a Miltown before we started. He slept part of the way. Got home at 1:30 A.M. Jack took another Miltown and slept till noon today. Just what he needed. Ruth is a good rock to have in all this. Business for the week was around $2,750. I was way off in my estimate.

May 25

Cooler and fair. Temperature will be in the 80s. In the 60s at night. I arose yesterday at about eight. I had breakfast on the patio—strolled about with Ruth, and sunned myself. Picked up a bit of a burn. Jack got up at noon. The *Tribune* and the *Times* did not use a picture that included Jack. This didn't seem to upset him. He left his golf clubs at our house, which reflects an unconscious optimism. How I do look for signs. Jack and I left for the city. Arrived at the Royale at 5:30 P.M. Ulu, wisely, had a run-through. They went at it leisurely and still gave it life. We lost the peaks, of course—but valleys I've never caught before became apparent as they relaxed. I invited them (only the actors and Ulu and I were there) to supper. Irene couldn't make it. We four went to Downey's. Ulu spoke of a few experiences as a refugee. And I found myself telling war experiences. A point in the script started me. Since I'd never done it before (with them), they were interested. I think I was trying to remind myself of times of real danger in an effort to minimize my present anxiety. Called Blanche when I got back to my room. She said Lucy Kroll was coming to the opening. After the call, I went to write something, and found that the pen that Lucy had given me was gone. What a coincidence—that a pen given me on the opening night of *Plowboy* should be lost on the eve of the opening of *Roses*. I was most upset. The call from Eddie Turro redeemed things. He told me that *Roses* moved him more than he supposed that any play could. Even discounting his personal involvement, that is quite a compliment. Dawn shared his feeling. They said they wanted me to know how they felt before the reviews. I fell asleep around 1:00 A.M. Woke at five. Dozed again till seven. How nervous am I? I never can tell. But I suspect I'm a lot more so than anyone seeing me would suspect. The physical fatigue of these past three months blunts all my feeling somewhat. That it's Monday is a damper. I have no intuition as to how we'll do. We deserve to do well—and we're capable of it. But my antenna is numb. Ulu says that regardless of what happens tonight, he is determined to do the play in a three-sided arena one day. so HERE IS THE DAY: perhaps I'll make entries from time to time today—a good way of easing my tension. Edgar just called me. He takes the day's weather as fair augury. All in control at his end. So?

Curtain up

Reviews

The *New York Herald Tribune,*
May 26, 1964,
by Walter Kerr

And some roses for Mr. Gilroy, please.

I'm sure you don't even want to hear about "The Subject Was Roses," let alone get up the energy to go see it. The season is late, and things are wrapped for the summer. The play has no stars to speak of, though it has actors to applaud. It has, as a matter of fact, only three actors, and that means just about what you imagine it does. The play is a small one, often a quiet one. But, if possible, clear your heads and pretend that late May and a low budget and no ballyhoo don't matter, for Frank Gilroy's "The Subject Was Roses" is quite the most interesting new American play to be offered on Broadway this season.

It is interesting because Mr. Gilroy is talented, not in the sense that he is promising but in the sense that he delivers absolutely everything he intends to. He intends to deliver a family triangle in which a father loves a son and a mother loves that son and the son loves both mother and father and not one of them can make a move or utter a sound that does not instantly damage the other. All right, it is a play of alienation, or, to use a less fashionable word, of estrangement, and whatever cosmic things are on one's mind can be read into it without much difficulty. But Mr. Gilroy's method as a writer is to let the cosmos go hang. He wants to be concrete.

What matters in his play is the storm that comes up from a lifetime of loveless living but comes up on Saturday morning because the waffles, made with the last egg in the house, stick to the griddle unexpectedly and on Sunday morning because the coffee is weak. The world is real to Mr. Gilroy, hard and unsupple and not subject to easy, pious manipulation. Drinks make a man drunk, blows in the face hurt, and the vehement spite with which a wife strikes away the husband who is clumsily and too late trying to seduce her is crude, cruel, and—beyond all reason, or perhaps for good reason—moving.

Director Ulu Grosbard, also making his Broadway debut, has sensed precisely the level of bland, blanching, hard-edged whisper at which his author means to convey an ordinary family's secrets, and he has held the stage-tone in near-perfect suspension. There are few open rows, and they are not the best of the battle. The best is in young Martin Sheen's face as he comes home from the wars—the time is 1946—to want to touch his mother but not to want her to touch him, as he stares across a table cluttered with beer cans into the too affable eyes of his father. He is referee here, and the object of the struggle besides, and what he does is to look hard and test.

He tests his power: his father will bring back to him the bottle of whiskey he wants to take away. He tests his charm: mother can be made to dance until the room spins, and, once he has rolled up a magazine and called to her through it as children do, he can unlock the door of her youth. He tests to see if there is any truth being spoken anywhere around him, destroying illusions about his conduct in battle (he has done everything he had to, and

volunteered for nothing), refusing to pity the crippled rela-
tive who has helped make an emotional cripple of his
mother, challenging each "kike" from his father's lips and
each Sunday-sentiment from his mother's. And all the time
hoping to heal what he must finally abandon.

Mr. Sheen is excellent. So is Jack Albertson, worrying
about what Father Reilly will say when his son doesn't
come to Mass; so is Irene Dailey, walking in equal, prede-
termined steps with her arms defeated at her sides. Neither
is a ghost. Both are tangible, well-meaning, obtuse, self-
pitying, vigorously angry realities, compounds of color, ac-
cumulations of past fact that cannot now be waved away.
Whatever does happen on the stage of the Royale happens
with finality.

As I say, not much happens. Three people face what
they are. But in the writing and in the staging there is an
economy of effect, a directness of tongue, together with a
simplicity of gesture, that very nearly opens the door to an
unexpected—but most plausible—poetry. In the first act,
late at night, the trio weave drowsily into their Bronx apartment after an uncustomary time on the town. The boy, in
the living room, suddenly remembers how much he loved
vaudeville. The parents, in the kitchen, are surprised to discover that they can remember the tune—and just a few
lines—of "Pretty Baby." The moods cross-breed on the
stage, and the moment is just a bit of a theatrical miracle.
In the second act, three sounds make a silence. The boy
spits a single word at his father, the father hits him hard
enough to topple him, and the mother is heard opening the
hallway door. The passage is a long, rhythmic, compounded
expletive; and we strain to hear what it doesn't say.

Too bad, really, that the prize-giving season is just over.
Small in outline as this occasion is, recognition is due in
every direction.

The *New York Times,*
May 26, 1964,
by Howard Taubman

Frank D. Gilroy has made good on the promise of "Who'll Save the Plowboy?" His new play, "The Subject Was Roses," which opened last night at the Royale Theater, is not only an impressive stride forward but also an honest and touching work in its own right.

Mr. Gilroy has not resorted to gimmicks, razzle-dazzle or advanced techniques to be in fashion. He has written a straightforward, realistic play that wears no airs. With simplicity, humor and integrity he has looked into the hearts of three decent people and discovered, by letting them discover, the feelings that divide and join them.

In "Who'll Save the Plowboy?," which was produced by the Phoenix Theater in 1962, Mr. Gilroy revealed that he had a refreshing awareness of the way ordinary-seeming men and women talk, think and feel but had not yet sharpened his dramatic style. "The Subject Was Roses" is evidence of marked progress, for it is written with economy and precision.

Although it is deceptively quiet in its reserve, "The Subject Was Roses" never loses a beat in its building of mood and conflict. It knows where it's going. It makes every line and gesture work and convey meaning. And at the end it has reached its destination, which, though no mountain peak, is at a raised plateau of perception.

It would have been easy to descend into bathos in this story of Timmy Cleary, a 21-year-old veteran, and his parents, to whose middle-class Bronx apartment he returns in 1946 after three years in the Army. But Mr. Gilroy knows the difference between sentiment and sentimentality, and he is not betrayed into the latter.

When the curtain rises on a Saturday morning, Jack Albertson as John Cleary is in the kitchen admiring his son's Eisenhower jacket with its corporal's stripes, its hash marks for overseas service and the infantryman's combat medal. There is a crude streamer on the adjoining living room wall welcoming Timmy home, and an upturned beer keg, draped in bunting, bears witness to the previous night's celebration for the returned warrior.

Irene Dailey as Nettie Cleary joins her husband in the kitchen, and there is an intimation that their relations are edgy. Mr. Gilroy does not labor his points. His touch is light, and he relies on his director, Ulu Grosbard, and his actors to flesh out the characters and to establish the atmosphere.

Miss Dailey's effort to make her son's favorite breakfast of waffles runs into trouble. Martin Sheen as the son who seems suddenly to hear and see everything afresh realizes that he has wounded her by not noting her concern. He coaxes his mother into dancing with him, and the taste of Miss Dailey's and Mr. Sheen's playing and of Mr. Grosbard's direction shed a glow on this scene.

The events of the 48 hours covering the play's action are not flashy. If one were to detail them, they would provide a bare outline. But each scene is another step in the education of the Clearys as they learn to face and accept truths about themselves.

Miss Dailey's Nettie is a luminous creation. She can suggest hurt and desiccation with a stricken glance. Wearing a plain hat and coat and holding her purse, she can turn to walk out of her apartment so that her back conveys her utter defeat and despair. In the one interlude that does not quite ring true—her recollection of her happy

99

youth—her tender reminiscence resolves all doubts in favor of the character.

Mr. Albertson plays the contrary and sentimental Irishman of a father with a fine mixture of truculence and self-pity. He has a tendency to slur his words, which made him difficult to follow early in the play, but when he speaks out, he is not only understandable but also vibrant.

Mr. Sheen's Timmy communicates an alert, attractive sense of newly won maturity. He knows how to listen to his parents so that he seems to reappraise their familiar phrases and attitudes before our very eyes. He has the skill to suggest independence without arrogance.

Credit Mr. Grosbard's sensitive, unobtrusive staging and Edgar Lansbury's scrupulously commonplace set as well as Mr. Gilroy for the dignity and warmth of this modest, truthful play. Don't these people know that it's flying in the face of tradition to bring in an honest work this late in May?

The *Daily News*,
May 26, 1964,
by John Chapman

"The Subject Was Roses," which was produced at the Royale Theatre last evening, is a low-key, kitchen-sink drama about a mother, father and war vet son who live in the Bronx and haven't got to know each other after all this time.

This is the first Broadway play by Frank D. Gilroy, a television writer who had an off-Broadway success a couple of years ago in "Who'll Save the Plowboy?" In "Roses" his three Irish characters are laconic enough to make the late Gary Cooper seem like a chatterbox. The dialog is filled with such naturalistic exchanges as "I wonder if it's still there." "I wonder." And "I couldn't sleep last night." "Neither could I."

And the director, Ulu Grosbard, a pupil at the Actors Studio, has been so bent on quiet naturalism that he makes each of his actors count two beats before saying "I wonder" or "Neither could I." Last evening, when a real toaster in the real kitchen popped up some real toast with utilitarian vigor, it surprised the audience and prompted it to laughter and applause.

Gilroy's intent has been a serious one, to write a play about three people, bound by the closest of human ties, who have remained strangers to each other—and to try to figure out why. His main trouble is, to me, that he has chosen three uninteresting characters to write about.

The father, played by Jack Albertson, at least raises his voice now and then, for he shows flashes of Irish temper between his grumpy, monosyllabic sulks. The son, played by Martin Sheen, is a listlessly cynical lad just returned from World War II who is listless even about getting drunk.

The mother, played by Irene Dailey, is a lifeless, discouraged and sexless woman whose only function is to make breakfast. Miss Dailey finally breaks into a long monologue in which she tries to tell her son what emotion it was that attracted her to his father those long years ago. This is the most moving scene in the drama—yet this scene, too, is unemotional, as though the wife doesn't care now about what happened.

The play is in eight scenes, starting with breakfast on Saturday morning, continuing with Sunday breakfast and ending with breakfast on Monday.

But the toaster goes off only once.

The *New York World-Telegram,*
May 26, 1964,
by Norman Nadel

From this day forth, Frank D. Gilroy is a major play-wright. The promise he showed in "Who'll Save the Plow-boy?," which was off-Broadway's best two seasons ago, has been fulfilled in "The Subject Was Roses," which opened last night at the Royale Theater. In this corner, the verdict is roses.

Gilroy has committed himself to excellence in this new family comedy-drama; the public will expect him to keep writing plays which will measure up to his own standard and which will be progressively broader in scope. The American theater needs Gilroy, and I judge from the ur-gency of his communication through the medium of the stage, that Gilroy needs the theater. Last night he gave us more than a fine and beautiful play; he also gave us the prospect of others to come.

In its externals, "The Subject Was Roses" is the sim-plest of plays; you are inclined to wonder at the beginning just how much strength can emanate from merely three characters and a single set.

Even the situation would seem to impose limits on the dramatist's resource. A 21-year-old son comes home to the Bronx after three years in the Army during World War II. He tries to adjust to his parents and they try to adjust to having him back. How far can you go with that?

To the most profound depths of the human heart; that's how far Gilroy takes us. Along the way he blends the humor and poignancy of family relationships into a play as beguiling as it is honest.

Martin Sheen portrays Timmy Cleary, the young man

who better understands his parents after the three-year absence than he ever did before. That which he previously observed—and reacted to—about them, he now can appraise in a more mature context.

Most playwrights (and actors) would make Timmy a rebel, building up a head of steam toward that moment when he'd rip his parents to shreds in an explosion of righteous resentment. Not here. Gilroy's Timmy knows about "Honor thy father and thy mother," and he's an affectionate, respectful son even when he's making them face up to their own pettiness and covert cruelty. Actor Sheen's Timmy is a boy not often seen on stage, but familiar in life.

There is no single dramatic explosion; the play builds more quietly, and if anything, more powerfully for the subtlety of its revelations.

Jack Albertson as the father and Irene Dailey as the mother reveal the most intimate insights in superbly detailed, yet wholly fluid and natural performances. She nurses her convenient psychic injury, inflicted by his infidelity, not realizing that the disease stems from something taught her long before she met him.

The father suffers her rejection, and nurses his own assortment of old guilt feelings—such as having been turned down for World War I service because he was the sole support of a family. He alternately covets his son's uniform and is angered by it as a reminder of his own failure to serve his country.

Gilroy's dialogue is so sensitive, so wise. The mother is crushed because the son had forgotten that waffles used to be his favorite breakfast. Her appraisal of her husband, in contrast to the baker from Paterson who also had courted her, has the clarity of poetry.

Ulu Grosbard directed "The Subject Was Roses" as if he had lived within the three people involved. For that matter,

Albertson, Sheen and Miss Dailey play it that way. I cannot imagine a line added or deleted, a gesture broadened or diminished. The production is just about perfect, which is no more than Gilroy's tender and lucid play deserves.

The *New York Post,*
May 26, 1964,
by Richard Watts, Jr.

Several years ago, Frank D. Gilroy revealed in "Who'll Save the Plowboy?" an impressive gift for unyielding dramatic realism. In his second play "The Subject Was Roses," which opened last night at the Royale Theater, he once more demonstrates his talent for sternly naturalistic writing, rather more assured in his powers and with incidental moments of wry humor added, in a harsh and relentless story of the crisis confronting a disturbed Irish-American family.

The skill of Mr. Gilroy within the bounds he has set for himself is striking. He has remarkable efficiency, never wasting a word and concentrating on what he has to say without a lost moment. He has an unfailing ear for dialogue, and every speech is unerring in its sound of actuality. And all three of his characters, a father, mother and war-veteran son, are observed with a ruthless credibility that is at the same time merciless and compassionate through understanding.

The father and mother have awaited their son's return eagerly, but his presence brings out the tension between them. Jealous of his affections, their emotions instinctively result in increasing recriminations, and the father's pride in his son is concealed in cruel and angry tirades. The son, who has a sense of guilt over knowing his sympathy for his mother has made him her ally against his father, turns on her with brutal words beyond his intentions.

In the end, the young man leaves home, and it is a logical ending, but it shows what seems to me Mr. Gilroy's prevailing weakness. The complete credibility of the three people and the remorseless conclusion can't conceal the disturbing fact that the resolution of his drama seems ineffectual. The truth about the family is there, and it is forcefully stated, but we have learned more of the tormented Clearys than we are told in the play's first half-hour.

If the work therefore seems to me more effective in its details than as a whole, the details are nonetheless striking. The title comes from the mother's love of roses. The son, knowing of his mother's feeling for them, buys her some and tells her they are from the father, but the husband, in an angry moment, admits the truth. It is one of the many revealing incidents, and I may be unfair in expecting some powerful climax in a play devoted to the strictest realism.

The three performances are notably fine. Irene Dailey is moving without ever being sentimental as the mother. Martin Sheen is admirably forceful as the son, and Jack Albertson brilliantly indicates the heart beneath the cantankerous speech of the father. Ulu Grosbard's expert staging is perhaps too muted for such a muted drama. If "The Subject Was Roses" lacks some of the final pointed insight beyond naturalism, it is still realism of a high order.

The *New York Journal-American,*
May 26, 1964,
by John McClain

Frank D. Gilroy, a television writer, stirred up a storm a couple of seasons ago with his "Who'll Save the Plowboy?," presented at the off-Broadway Phoenix Theatre.

This was his first shot at drama and it was generally agreed at the time that he was carrying quite a load of talent and should be heard from in the future.

So last night he bobbed up on Broadway and the Royale Theatre with a new play, "The Subject Was Roses," and despite the fact that the three-character drama came to town as one of the best-kept secrets of the season, I believe it justified the prediction that he has extraordinary gifts as a dramatist.

He has a marvelous ear for dialogue, can create interesting and valid characters and maneuver them into compelling situations. What he can't do, apparently, is resolve the problems he sets for himself.

An old axiom in the playwriting racket insists that characters in the successful drama must show progression or recession in the course of an evening and that, in my opinion, is what keeps "Roses" from being a much stronger play than it presently is.

We come upon a mother and father welcoming their only son back from service in World War II.

It develops slowly and with effective small scenes that the wife has long since fallen out of love with her husband, that the husband believes his wife and son are united against him, and that the wife feels her husband does not appreciate their boy.

There is also the familiar failure of all three to communicate with one another, and even the lad himself, torn between his sincere affection for both his parents, can find no better solution in the end than merely moving out on both of them.

It must be said for the skill of the author that we come to know these three people very well and feel a strenuous interest in what happens to them. Which makes it all the more deplorable that they wind up as far apart as when we first encountered them.

This may be an entirely valid slice of life, raw and uncompromising and often extremely moving, but it does not result in a very rewarding evening for the customers.

Beyond the humor and poignancy of the writing are the magnificent performances of Jack Albertson, as the father; Irene Dailey, as the mother, and Martin Sheen, as the son —and the tasteful and unostentatious direction of Ulu Grosbard. Yes, Ulu Grosbard.

It appeared to me that the rather scanty first night audience had arrived reluctantly to witness something less than a smash and had remained to rejoice in an experience of unexpected merit.

Meritorious as it certainly is, I doubt that it has the popular appeal to register as a big hit. But it again reveals Mr. Gilroy's exceptional promise as a playwright, and the fact that this one may not come up roses should not dull his ambition.

THE *ROSES* COMPANY
STATEMENT OF PRODUCTION COSTS
(*to first preview, May 18, 1964*)

SCENERY & PROPS		
Building set	$ 4,275.00	
Props & furniture	360.65	
Scrim	374.40	$ 5,010.05
WARDROBE		542.94
ELECTRIC & SOUND		328.91
FEES		
Director	2,000.00	
Designers		
Scenic	1,175.00	
Lighting	587.50	
Wardrobe	250.00	4,012.50
REHEARSAL		
Salaries		
Actors	1,170.00	
Stage managers	907.30	
Crew	575.00	
Wardrobe	41.67	
General & company managers	1,200.00	
Transportation	337.89	
New York living expenses	600.00	
Stage manager expenses	100.00	
Production assistant	100.00	
Departmental		
Property	87.20	
Electric	38.37	
Carpenter	45.42	
Miscellaneous	138.05	5,340.90

PUBLICITY

Press agent salary & expense	1,060.00	
Share newspaper advertisements	1,693.67	
Printing & mailing	534.82	
Photos & signs	1,014.24	4,302.73

OTHER

Legal fees & expenses	1,195.71	
Legal advertising	407.30	
Accounting	175.00	
Take in & set up	1,282.65	
Hauling	290.00	
Theatre salaries		
(Box office & dress rehearsal)	865.39	
Miscellaneous & casting	239.19	
Payroll taxes	271.00	
Insurance & hospitalization	175.00	4,901.24

TOTAL PRODUCTION COSTS

	$ 24,439.27

Returnable bonds		
Actors Equity Union	$ 4,000.00	
IATSE Union	1,116.00	
ATPAM Union	1,000.00	
Theatrical Wardrobe Union	250.00	
Theatre bond	5,000.00	
Total returnable bonds		$11,366.00
Advances on expenses		
Insurance, hospitalization		
& miscellaneous	302.80	
Equipment rentals	1,249.20	
Total advances on expenses		1,552.00
Production costs		
As per above		$24,439.27

TOTAL FUNDS DISBURSED:

	$37,357.27

Epilogue

We opened with a $165 advance sale; registered substantial losses until our fourth week; borrowed some $10,000; received invaluable aid and encouragement from many people (too many to name) who made a cause of our survival.

We did not have a sold-out house until our 136th performance.

We moved to the Winthrop Ames Theatre on September 7, 1964, and intend to run (as Jack puts it) "until we do it right."

The Subject Was Roses

THE SUBJECT WAS ROSES

was first presented by Edgar Lansbury *at the Royale Theatre, New York City, on May 25, 1964, with the following cast:*

(IN ORDER OF APPEARANCE)

JOHN CLEARY	Jack Albertson
NETTIE CLEARY	Irene Dailey
TIMMY CLEARY	Martin Sheen

Directed by Ulu Grosbard
Scenery designed by Edgar Lansbury
Lighting by Jules Fisher
Costumes by Donald Foote
Production stage manager: Paul Leaf

Synopsis of Scenes

ACT ONE

A middle-class apartment.
May 1946.

Scene 1: Saturday morning
Scene 2: Saturday afternoon
Scene 3: Two A.M. Monday morning

ACT TWO

The same place.

Scene 1: Sunday morning
Scene 2: Sunday evening
Scene 3: Two A.M. Monday morning
Scene 4: Nine A.M. Monday morning

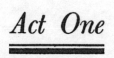

Act One

Scene 1

Scene: The kitchen and living room of a middle-class apartment in the West Bronx. A doorway links the two rooms; an invisible wall divides them. The living room is furnished with the heavy upholstered pieces (replete with antimacassars) considered fashionable in the late twenties and early thirties. There is evidence of a party given the night before: a beer keg, a stack of camp chairs, a sagging banner that is hand lettered—"Welcome Home, Timmy."

Time: A Saturday morning in May of 1946.

At rise: A man stands alone in the kitchen, lost in contemplation of an army jacket hanging from the door. The man, JOHN CLEARY, is fifty. The army jacket bears an infantry division patch, corporal chevrons, service ribbons (including the ETO with two battle stars, and a presidential unit citation), four "Hershey Bars" marking two years of overseas duty, and the "Ruptured Duck" signifying recent discharge. JOHN CLEARY's expression as he regards the jacket is one of almost reverent curiosity. He touches the jacket, feels the material, traces the outline of the chevrons inquiringly. Now, on an impulse, he takes the jacket from the hanger, dons it furtively, is enjoying what is obviously a secret moment when he hears a key turn in the front door. Quickly returning the jacket to the hanger, he takes a seat at the kitchen table and appears engrossed in a newspaper as the door opens and his wife, NETTIE, forty-five, enters with a bundle of groceries.

NETTIE   It's a lovely day . . . Timmy still asleep?

JOHN   Haven't heard him . . . Better give me mine.

NETTIE   I thought we'd all have breakfast together.

JOHN   I have to go downtown.

NETTIE   Today?

JOHN   Ruskin wants to see me. (*She regards him a moment, then begins to set the food before him*) I'm going to stop at St. Francis on the way . . . to offer a prayer of thanks.

NETTIE   Toast?

JOHN   Yes . . . All those casualties and he never got a scratch. We're very lucky.

NETTIE   What do you want on it?

JOHN   Marmalade . . . The Freeman boy dead. The Mullin boy crippled for life . . . Makes you wonder . . . Think he enjoyed the party?

NETTIE   He seemed to.

JOHN   First time I ever saw him take a drink.

NETTIE   He drank too much.

JOHN   You don't get out of the army every day.

NETTIE   He was sick during the night.

JOHN   Probably the excitement.

NETTIE   It was the whiskey. You should have stopped him.

JOHN   For three years he's gotten along fine without anyone telling him what to do.

NETTIE   I had to hold his head.

JOHN   No one held his head in the army.

NETTIE   That's what *he* said.

JOHN   But that didn't stop *you*.

NETTIE   He's not in the army any more.

JOHN   It was a boy that walked out of this house three years ago. It's a man that's come back in.

NETTIE   You sound like a recruiting poster.

JOHN   *You* sound ready to repeat the old mistakes.

NETTIE   Mistakes?

JOHN   Pardon me.

NETTIE   You said mistakes.

JOHN   Slip of the tongue.

NETTIE   I'd like to know what mistakes you're referring to.

JOHN   The coffee's excellent.

NETTIE   I'd really like to know.

JOHN   He was eighteen when he went away. Until that time, he showed no special skill at anything, but you treated him like he was a protégé.

NETTIE   I think you mean prodigy.

JOHN   What I really mean is baby.

NETTIE   For a baby he certainly did well in the army.

JOHN   I didn't say he *was* a baby. I said you treated him like one.

NETTIE   You were surprised he did well. You didn't think he'd last a week.

JOHN   Bless us and save us, said Mrs. O'Davis.

NETTIE   Do you know why you were surprised?

JOHN   Joy, joy, said Mrs. Malloy.

NETTIE   Because you never understood him.

JOHN   Mercy, mercy, said old Mrs. Percy.

NETTIE   I never doubted that he'd do as well as anyone else.

JOHN   Where he's concerned you never doubted, period. If he came in here right now and said he could fly, you'd help him out the window.

NETTIE   If you're saying I have confidence in him, you're right. And why not? Who knows him better?

JOHN   Is there more coffee?

NETTIE   He's exceptional.

JOHN   Here we go again.

NETTIE   Yes—exceptional!

JOHN   In what way?

NETTIE   I refuse to discuss it.

JOHN   A person who's going to be famous usually drops a *few* clues by the time they're twenty-one.

NETTIE   I didn't say famous—I said exceptional.

JOHN   What's the difference?

NETTIE   You wouldn't understand.

JOHN   Here's something you better understand—you can't treat him as though he'd never been away. He's not a kid.

NETTIE   If you had stopped him from drinking too much that would have been treating him like a kid?

JOHN   This is where I came in.

NETTIE   He was trying to keep up with you and you knew it.

JOHN You sound like you're jealous.

NETTIE The two of you so busy drinking you hardly paid attention to anyone else.

JOHN You *are* jealous!

NETTIE Don't be absurd.

JOHN He and I got along better yesterday than we ever did before and you're jealous. (*She turns away*) Well, well, well.
(*He finishes the last of his coffee. Rises to leave*)

NETTIE Can't Ruskin wait till Monday?

JOHN No. And don't pretend you're disappointed. What a charming little breakfast you and he will have together.

NETTIE You're welcome to stay.

JOHN My ears are burning already.

NETTIE I've never said a word against you and you know it.

JOHN Don't forget my excursion to Montreal.

NETTIE It was always your own actions that turned him against you.

JOHN And the convention—don't leave that out.
(*He starts from the room*)

NETTIE The curtains. (*He regards her*) The curtains for Timmy's room. They're coming today.

JOHN I don't know anything about curtains.

NETTIE Yes, you do.

JOHN I do not.

NETTIE They'll be ten dollars.

JOHN   What's the matter with the old ones?
      (TIMMY CLEARY, *twenty-one, wearing army sun-*
      tans, open at the neck, emerges from his room,
      starts toward the kitchen, is arrested by their voices.
      He stops, listens)

NETTIE   They're worn out.

JOHN   They look all right to me.

NETTIE   They aren't all right.

JOHN   Ten dollars for curtains.

NETTIE   Timmy will want to bring friends home.

JOHN   The old squeeze play.
      (TIMMY *puts his hands over his ears*)

NETTIE   Are you going to give me the money?
      (JOHN *extracts a bill from his wallet, slaps it on the*
      table)

JOHN   Here!

NETTIE   I need five dollars for the house.

JOHN   I gave you fifteen yesterday.

NETTIE   That went for the party.

JOHN   That party cost close to a hundred dollars.

NETTIE   It was worth it.

JOHN   Did I say it wasn't? (*He takes another bill from his*
      wallet and puts it down) There.
      (TIMMY *goes back, slams the door of his room to*
      alert them, then approaches the kitchen. NETTIE *and*
      JOHN *compose themselves cheerfully as* TIMMY,
      equally cheerful, enters)

TIMMY   Good morning.

JOHN   Champ.

126

NETTIE Morning, son.
(TIMMY *shakes hands with his father; kisses his mother on the cheek*)

JOHN We thought you were going to sleep all day.

TIMMY I smelled the coffee.

JOHN Mother said you were sick during the night.

TIMMY I'm fine now.

JOHN I was a little rocky myself.

TIMMY I wonder why.
(*They both laugh*)

NETTIE (*To* JOHN) What time is your appointment?

JOHN Eleven-fifteen.

NETTIE It's twenty-five of.

JOHN (*To* TIMMY) Mr. Ruskin wants to see me.

TIMMY That's too bad.

JOHN Why?

TIMMY Thought we might take in the Giant game.

NETTIE (*To* JOHN) Why don't you?

JOHN You know I can't. (*To* TIMMY) This thing with Ruskin means a sure sale.

TIMMY I understand.

JOHN We'll go tomorrow.

NETTIE My mother expects us for dinner tomorrow.
(JOHN *looks at* NETTIE *as though he might say something, thinks better of it, turns to* TIMMY)

JOHN How about *next* Saturday?

TIMMY   All right.

JOHN   We'll get box seats—the works.

TIMMY   Sounds fine.

JOHN   Swell.

NETTIE   What time will you be home?

JOHN   I'll call you.

NETTIE   I'll be at my mother's.

JOHN   (*Appraising* TIMMY)   I understand none of your old clothes fit.

TIMMY   That's right.

JOHN   Meet me downtown on Monday and we'll get you some new ones.

TIMMY   Okay.
(JOHN *feints a jab.* TIMMY *covers up. They spar good-naturedly until* TIMMY *drops his hands*)

JOHN   I still think I can take you.

TIMMY   I wouldn't be surprised.

JOHN   See you later.

TIMMY   Right.
(JOHN *moves toward the door, stops before the army jacket, indicates one of the ribbons*)

JOHN   What did you say this one was for?

TIMMY   It's a combat infantry badge.

JOHN   How about that?

TIMMY   It's not as important as it sounds.

JOHN   We'll have to sit down and have a real talk. I want to hear all about it.

TIMMY   All right.

JOHN   It's great to have you home.

TIMMY   It's great to be home.

JOHN   The Mullin boy crippled. The Freeman boy dead. We're very lucky.

TIMMY   I know.

JOHN   I'm stopping off at St. Francis this morning to offer a prayer of thanks . . . See you later.

TIMMY   Right.
(JOHN *exits from the apartment.* TIMMY *looks after him*)

NETTIE   How did you sleep?

TIMMY   Fine . . . How's he feeling?

NETTIE   All right.

TIMMY   He looks a lot older.

NETTIE   It's been two years . . . It must have seemed strange. (*He glances at her*) Sleeping in your own bed.

TIMMY   (*Turning away again*)   Yes . . . How's his business?

NETTIE   Who knows?

TIMMY   The coffee market's off.

NETTIE   I hope you're hungry.

TIMMY   I can't get over the change in him.

NETTIE   Guess what we're having for breakfast.

TIMMY   It's not just the way he looks.

NETTIE   *Guess what we're having for breakfast.* (*He turns to her*) Guess what we're having.

TIMMY   What?

NETTIE   Guess.

TIMMY   I don't know.

NETTIE   Yes, you do.

TIMMY   No.

NETTIE   Sure you do.

TIMMY   What is it?

NETTIE   You're fooling.

TIMMY   What is it?

NETTIE   What's your favorite?

TIMMY   Bacon and eggs?

NETTIE   Now I know you're fooling.

TIMMY   No.

NETTIE   I forgot what a tease you were.

TIMMY   I'm not teasing.

NETTIE   Waffles. We're having waffles.

TIMMY   Fine.

NETTIE   You used to be crazy about waffles.

TIMMY   I still am.

NETTIE   I've got the waffle batter ready.

TIMMY   Swell.

NETTIE   Your first morning home, you're entitled to whatever you want.

TIMMY   I want waffles.

NETTIE   I used the last egg in the batter.

TIMMY   *I want waffles.*

NETTIE   Really?

TIMMY   Cross my heart.

NETTIE   All right.
(*While she prepares things, he goes to a window, gazes out*)

TIMMY   I see a new butcher.

NETTIE   Quite a few new stores.

TIMMY   Pop said the Bremens moved.

NETTIE   And the Costellos . . . Remember old Zimmer the tailor?

TIMMY   Sure.

NETTIE   A few weeks ago a woman brought him a coat she wanted altered. Zimmer started to fix it, then very politely excused himself, went up to the roof and jumped. No one knows why.

TIMMY   Who was the woman?

NETTIE   Mrs. Levin.

TIMMY   That explains it.

NETTIE   That's not funny.

TIMMY   Sorry.

NETTIE   What a thing to say.

TIMMY   I said I'm sorry.

NETTIE   I'm surprised at you.

TIMMY   Bless us and save us.

NETTIE *What?*

TIMMY Bless us and save us. As in "Bless us and save us, said Mrs. O'Davis; Joy, joy, said Mrs. Malloy . . ." (*She regards him incredulously*) What's the matter?

NETTIE I never expected to hear that nonsense from *you!*

TIMMY It beats swearing.

NETTIE You used to cover your ears when your father said it.

TIMMY (*With mock solemnity*) I'll never say it again.

NETTIE *Don't talk to me like that!* . . . I'm sorry. I don't know what's wrong with me this morning. I don't think I slept well . . . Too much excitement—the party and all. (*She resumes the preparation of breakfast: pours batter on the waffle iron while he, still not recovered from her outburst, studies her*) Will you have bacon with it?

TIMMY Just the waffles will be fine.

NETTIE Did you like the party?

TIMMY Yes.

NETTIE I wish the house had looked better.

TIMMY What's wrong with it?

NETTIE It needs painting. The sofa's on its last legs. And the rugs . . . Well, now that you're here I'll get it all fixed up.

TIMMY It looks fine to me.

NETTIE I still can't believe you're here.

TIMMY I find it a little hard to believe myself.

NETTIE You *are* here?

TIMMY Want to pinch me? . . . Go ahead. (*She hesitates. He holds out his hand*) Go on. (*She takes his hand*) Believe it now? (*She continues to hold his hand. He becomes uneasy*) Hey. (*Oblivious to his resistance, she still clings to his hand*) What are you doing? (*She persists. His agitation mounts*) Cut it out . . . Cut it out! (*He jerks free of her; immediately tries to make light of it*) One pinch to a customer . . . House rule. (*She regards him mutely*) The waffles must be ready; the light on the iron went out. (*She just looks at him*) Isn't that what it means when that little light goes out? (*She looks at him a moment more, then goes to the waffle iron, lifts the cover, starts to remove the waffles, stops, moves to a chair, sits, folds her hands in her lap and begins to cry*) What's the matter? . . . What's wrong? . . . What is it? . . . *What is it?*

NETTIE (*Continuing to cry*) They stuck.

TIMMY What?

NETTIE Why did they have to stick today?

TIMMY The waffles?

NETTIE I can't remember the last time they stuck.

TIMMY What's that to cry about?

NETTIE I've looked forward to this morning for three years and nothing's right.

TIMMY Why do you say that?

NETTIE Not one thing.

TIMMY What isn't right?

NETTIE Not one single thing.

TIMMY Will you please stop?

NETTIE   The things you've been saying—your attitude.

TIMMY   What things? What attitude?

NETTIE   You haven't even asked about Willis.

TIMMY   . . . How is he?

NETTIE   Every time I look at you, you avoid me.

TIMMY (*Turning away*)   That's ridiculous.

NETTIE   You're doing it now.

TIMMY   I am not!

NETTIE   How could you forget waffles were your favorite?

TIMMY   I just forgot.

NETTIE   Then you must have forgotten a lot of things.

TIMMY   *I'll tell you one thing I didn't forget.* (*She looks at him*) The dance. (*No reaction from her*) The one we were going to have the first morning I was home.

NETTIE   What made you think of that?

TIMMY   It's been on my mind all along.

NETTIE   I'll bet.

TIMMY   I was about to turn the radio on when you started crying.

NETTIE   I'll bet.

TIMMY   If you're through, I'll do it now. Are you through?

NETTIE   I haven't danced in so long I've probably forgotten how.
   (*He goes to the living room, snaps on the radio, dials to a band playing a slow fox trot, returns to the kitchen*)

TIMMY Shall we have a go at it?

NETTIE I can't remember the last time I danced.

TIMMY Come on.

NETTIE You really want to?

TIMMY Yes.

NETTIE (*Rising*) You asked for it.

TIMMY That-a-girl. (*He puts his arms about her*) Here
we go. (*They move smoothly, gracefully*) Forgot how
to dance—who you kidding?

NETTIE I guess it's one of those things you never forget.

TIMMY Remember this? (*He goes into a maneuver that
she follows perfectly*) You've been taking lessons.

NETTIE Of course.
(*They dance from the kitchen into the living
room*)

TIMMY Come here off-ten?

NETTIE Foist time.

TIMMY Me likewise . . . By yuhself?

NETTIE Widda goil friend.
(*The song ends*)

ANNOUNCER'S VOICE That's all the time we have on Dance
Parade this morning. I hope—
(*TIMMY goes to the radio, dials, picks up a polka
band going full blast*)

TIMMY What do you say?

NETTIE The spirit's willing.

TIMMY Let's go! (*They take off*) Not bad . . . not bad.

NETTIE   What will the neighbors think?

TIMMY   The worst. (*The rhythm begins to accelerate*)
We're coming into the home stretch. Hang on.
(*They move faster and faster*)

NETTIE   I'm getting dizzy.
(*As they whirl about the room they begin to laugh*)

TIMMY   Hang on.

NETTIE   I can't do any more.
(*The laughter grows*)

TIMMY   Hang on!

NETTIE   I can't!
(*The laughter becomes hysterical*)

TIMMY   Hang on! Hang on!

NETTIE   I can't! I . . .
(*They trip, collapse to the floor*)

TIMMY   You all right?

NETTIE   I think so.
(*Both breathe laboredly. The laughter subsides. He
snaps the radio off, then sits on the floor facing her*)

TIMMY   I'm dead . . . absolutely dead.

NETTIE   So am I.

TIMMY   I can't remember the last time I laughed like that.

NETTIE   I can . . . We were driving to the lake and
stopped at that dinky carnival.

TIMMY   The time I got you to go on that ride.

NETTIE   Your father thought we'd lost our minds. He kept
begging the man to stop the engine.

TIMMY Which made us laugh all the harder.

NETTIE Know something?

TIMMY What?

NETTIE I really believe you're here now.

TIMMY So do I.

NETTIE What are you going to do today?

TIMMY I don't know.

NETTIE Why don't you come to Mama's with me?

TIMMY We're going there for dinner tomorrow.

NETTIE Willis would love to see you.

TIMMY I'll see him tomorrow.

NETTIE When we told him you were coming home he began to sing. It's the first time he's done that in months.

TIMMY All right, I'll go.

NETTIE We won't stay long.

TIMMY All right.
(*The door opens and* JOHN *enters, sees them on the floor*)

JOHN Well, hello. (TIMMY *rises*) Don't get up on my account.

TIMMY We were dancing and fell down.

NETTIE (*To* JOHN) What did you forget?

JOHN Nothing.

NETTIE (*Rising*) Why did you come back?

JOHN I changed my mind. (*To* TIMMY) If you still want to go to the ball game, it's a date.

137

NETTIE   What about Ruskin?

JOHN   The hell with him. (*To* TIMMY) Still want to go?

TIMMY   Yes.

NETTIE   What about Willis?

JOHN   What *about* Willis?

NETTIE   Timmy was going to see him this afternoon.

TIMMY   I'll see him tomorrow.

NETTIE   I told him you'd be over today.

TIMMY   Before you even asked me?

NETTIE   I thought sure you'd want to.

TIMMY   You had no right to do that.

NETTIE   What will I tell him?

TIMMY   Tell him I'll be there tomorrow.

NETTIE   He'll be disappointed.

TIMMY   That's not my fault.

JOHN   The game starts at twelve.

TIMMY   Just have to get my tie.

NETTIE   You haven't eaten.

TIMMY   We'll grab something on the way.
  (*He exits*)

JOHN   I came out of St. Francis and started for the subway. Was halfway there when I thought of Mr. Freeman: What wouldn't *he* give to be able to spend a day
  with his son? . . . It made me turn around and come
  back. (*She just looks at him*) You're mad. (*No reply*)
  You told me to take him to the game.

NETTIE And you always do what I tell you.

JOHN Bless us and save us.
(TIMMY, *knotting his tie, reappears, puts on his jacket, snaps to attention*)

TIMMY Corporal Cleary reporting for duty.

JOHN Kiss your mother good-bye.

TIMMY That's not a duty. (*He kisses* NETTIE *on the cheek. She receives the kiss impassively*) So long, Mom.

JOHN We won't be late.
(*He and* TIMMY *exit. She stands as she is*)
                    Curtain

Scene 2

Time: Late afternoon—the same day.

At rise: JOHN *and* TIMMY *enter the apartment.* TIMMY *carries a bouquet of red roses.* JOHN *has just concluded a joke and they are both laughing.*

JOHN   I haven't told that one in years.

TIMMY   I was considered a very funny fellow. Thanks to you.

JOHN   Hello? . . . Anybody home? (*No answer*) Still at her mother's.

TIMMY   (*Indicating the roses*) I better put these in water.
    (*They move into the kitchen*)

JOHN   Stand another beer?

TIMMY   Sure.
    (*While* TIMMY *puts the roses in a vase,* JOHN *gets two cans of beer from the refrigerator*)

JOHN   (*Opening the beers*) How did you remember all those jokes of mine?

TIMMY   Just came to me.

JOHN   I don't remember most of them myself . . . (*Hands* TIMMY *a beer*) Here you go.

TIMMY   Thanks.

JOHN   What'll we drink to?

TIMMY   The Chicago Cubs.

JOHN   Think it'll help them?

Martin Sheen, Irene Dailey and Jack Albertson as
TIMMY CLEARY, NETTIE CLEARY and JOHN CLEARY

TIMMY Can it hurt?

JOHN (*Raising the can*) To the Cubs.

TIMMY To the Cubs.
(*They both drink*)

JOHN Sixteen to three.

TIMMY I'm still glad we went.

JOHN So am I. (*Drinks*) That was a beautiful catch Ott made.

TIMMY Yes.

JOHN For a moment I thought he lost it in the sun. (*TIMMY says nothing.* JOHN *drinks*) So they really went for the old man's jokes?

TIMMY Especially the ones about Uncle Mike.

JOHN Such as?

TIMMY The Pennsylvania Hotel gag.

JOHN Columbus told that one to the Indians.

TIMMY Uncle Mike was a famous man in our outfit.

JOHN Joking aside, he was quite a guy. Stood six three. Weighed close to two fifty.

TIMMY I remember his picture.

JOHN He was in the Spanish American War.

TIMMY I know.

JOHN Got hit by a bullet once that knocked him out. When he came to, he was lying in a field full of wounded men. The ones that were sure goners were marked with yellow tags so no one would waste time on them. The others had blue tags. Mike found a yellow tag around his wrist. The fellow next to him who was unconscious had a blue one. Quick as a wink Mike switched the tags and . . . How about that? I'm telling *you* war stories. Go on—you do the talking.

TIMMY About what?

JOHN You must have seen some pretty bad things.

TIMMY Not as much as a lot of others.

JOHN Maybe you'd rather not talk about it.

TIMMY I don't mind.

JOHN I'd like to hear what you have to say.

TIMMY I don't know how to begin.

JOHN Anything that comes to mind.

TIMMY Want to hear the bravest thing I ever did?

JOHN Yes.

TIMMY The first night we were in combat I slept with my boots off.

JOHN Go on.

TIMMY That's it.

JOHN You slept with your boots off?

TIMMY Doesn't sound like much, does it?

JOHN Not offhand.

TIMMY The fellows who eventually cracked up were all guys who couldn't sleep. If I hadn't decided to take my boots off I'd have ended up being one of them.

JOHN I see.

TIMMY Want to know the smartest thing I did?

JOHN Sure.

TIMMY I never volunteered. One day the lieutenant bawled me out for it. I said, "Sir, if there's anything you want me to do, you tell me and I'll do it. But if you wait for me to volunteer you'll wait forever."

JOHN What did he say to that?

TIMMY Nothing printable. The fact is I wasn't a very good soldier, Pop.

JOHN You did everything they asked you.

TIMMY The good ones do more. You'd have been a good one.

JOHN What makes you say that?

TIMMY I can tell.

JOHN Well, thanks.

TIMMY You're welcome.

JOHN It's one of the big regrets of my life that I was never in the service.

TIMMY I know.

JOHN The day World War One was declared I went to the recruiting office. When they learned I was the sole support of the family, they turned me down.

TIMMY I know.

JOHN A lot of people made cracks. Especially guys like Clayton and Harper who waited to be drafted and then wangled safe jobs at Governor's Island and the Navy Yard . . . I fixed their wagons one night—sent the army flying one way and the navy the other. That was the last about slacking I heard from *them* . . . Still it bothers

me—missing out on the whole thing . . . I keep won-
dering what difference it might have made in my life
. . . And then I wonder how I'd have made out . . . I
wouldn't have settled for a desk job. I'd have gotten to
the front.

TIMMY   I'm sure of that.

JOHN   But once there, how would I have done?

TIMMY   Fine.

JOHN   How do you know?

TIMMY   You're a born fighter.

JOHN   They say a lot of fellows who were terrors as civil-
ians turned to jelly when they heard those bullets.

TIMMY   Not you.

JOHN   It doesn't seem so. But you can't be sure . . .
That's always bothered me. (*Drinks the last of his beer*)
How about another?

TIMMY   Fine.

JOHN   Maybe we shouldn't.

TIMMY   Why?

JOHN   Your mother blames me for your getting sick last
night; says I encouraged you to drink too much.

TIMMY   It wasn't what I drank. It was the excitement.

JOHN   That's what I told her.

TIMMY   *I'll* open two more.

JOHN   All right. (*While* TIMMY *gets the beers,* JOHN *regards the roses*) Her father used to send her roses every
birthday . . . A dozen red ones . . . Never missed . . .
Even at the end.

TIMMY Tell her they were your idea.

JOHN What?

TIMMY Tell her the roses were your idea.

JOHN Why?

TIMMY She'll get a kick out of it . . . All right?

JOHN If you like.

TIMMY (*Handing him a beer*) Here you go.

JOHN Thanks.

TIMMY You call it this time.

JOHN (*Raising his beer*) To the two nicest fellows in the house.

TIMMY I'll buy that. (*They drink.* TIMMY *regards the can*) Funny how you acquire a taste for things.

JOHN Yes.

TIMMY When I was a kid I couldn't even stand the smell of beer.

JOHN Believe it or not I was the same.

TIMMY We seem to have gotten over it.

JOHN Yes . . . Can I say something to you?

TIMMY Sure.

JOHN You won't take it the wrong way?

TIMMY No.

JOHN I owe you an apology.

TIMMY For what?

JOHN You were always sick; always home from school

145

with one thing or another. I never thought you'd last in the army.

TIMMY   Neither did I.

JOHN   Really?

TIMMY   Really.

JOHN   When Dr. Goldman heard they took you he said it was ridiculous. When they put you in the infantry he said it was inhuman.

TIMMY   And when I survived?

JOHN   He said it was a miracle. (*They both laugh*) I don't think it was a miracle. I think we just underestimated you . . . Especially me . . . That's what I wanted to apologize for.

TIMMY   Remember that corny thing you used to recite— about how a boy thinks his father is the greatest guy in the world until he's fifteen. Then the doubts start. By the time he's eighteen he's convinced his father is the worst guy in the world. At twenty-five the doubts start again. At thirty it occurs to him that the old man wasn't so bad after all. At forty—

JOHN   What about it?

TIMMY   There's some truth to it.

JOHN   I think you've had too much to drink.

TIMMY   I'm not saying you're a saint.

JOHN   That's a relief.

TIMMY   But taking into account where you started from, and the obstacles you had to overcome, what you've done is something to be proud of.

JOHN Well, thank you.

TIMMY How many guys that you grew up with even turned out legitimate?

JOHN Not many.

TIMMY And most of *them* are still scraping along where they started.

JOHN That's true.

TIMMY How many years of school did you have?

JOHN I had to quit after the fourth grade.

TIMMY I've met college graduates who don't know nearly as much as you about the things that really count.

JOHN Must have been Yale men.

TIMMY I'm serious.

JOHN Speaking of college . . . If you get into one of those big ones and it's more than the G.I. Bill pays for, I'll help you out.

TIMMY Thanks.

JOHN That's just between you and me.

TIMMY Why?

JOHN I don't want people getting wrong notions.

TIMMY About what?

JOHN That I'm loaded.

TIMMY *Are* you loaded?

JOHN Don't be ridiculous.

TIMMY That doesn't answer my question.

JOHN The question's ridiculous.

TIMMY That's still no answer.

JOHN No, I'm not loaded.

TIMMY How much do you have?

JOHN What?

TIMMY How much money do you have?

JOHN Is this your idea of a joke?

TIMMY No.

JOHN Then why are you doing it?

TIMMY I don't want to take money from you if you can't afford it.

JOHN I can afford it.

TIMMY Some of the places I applied at are pretty expensive.

JOHN I can afford it!

TIMMY Then you must be loaded.

JOHN *I am not loaded!*

TIMMY We have a summer place, a car. Now you tell me you can afford any school in the country. You must be fairly loaded.

JOHN *If I hear that word once more, I'm marching right out the door!*
(TIMMY *is unable to suppress his laughter any longer*)

TIMMY You haven't changed a bit. (JOHN *regards him uncertainly*) You look as though I'd asked you to betray your country.
(JOHN, *against his will, smiles*)

JOHN   You son of a gun.

TIMMY   I really had you going.

JOHN   Some joke.

TIMMY   Oh, say, Pop.

JOHN   What?

TIMMY   How much *do* you have?

JOHN   *Enough's enough!* (TIMMY *laughs anew*) I think we better change the subject.

TIMMY   How did you meet Mother? (JOHN *regards him*) You said change the subject.

JOHN   You know all about that.

TIMMY   Just that you picked her up on the subway.

JOHN   It wasn't like that at all.

TIMMY   Then I don't know all about it.

JOHN   "Picked her up" makes it sound cheap.

TIMMY   Sorry.

JOHN   The first time I spoke to her was on the subway but there's more to it.

TIMMY   Tell me.

JOHN   Why?

TIMMY   I might become a writer and want to do a story about it someday.

JOHN   A writer?

TIMMY   Maybe.

JOHN   Well, that's the first I heard about that.

149

TIMMY   Me, too. Must be the beer . . . What year was it you met her?

JOHN   Nineteen twenty-one . . . A writer?

TIMMY   A writer . . . Where were you working then?

JOHN   At Emerson's . . .

TIMMY   And?

JOHN   One morning I saw her walk by. That afternoon she passed again. Same the next day. Turned out she worked around the corner. I . . . You sure you want to hear this?

TIMMY   Uh-huh.

JOHN   One evening I happened to be leaving at the same time she did. Turned out we took the same subway. She got off at Seventy-second Street . . . To make a long story short, I got a seat next to her one day and we started talking.

TIMMY   That's it?

JOHN   Yes.

TIMMY   Sounds like an ordinary pickup to me.

JOHN   *Well, it wasn't* . . . I left some things out.

TIMMY   Such as?

JOHN   I don't remember . . . It was twenty-five years ago.

TIMMY   The way I heard it, you followed her for a month before you finally got the nerve to speak.

JOHN   I thought you didn't know the story.

TIMMY   To convince her your intentions were honorable,

you asked if you might call at her home. True or false?
. . . Well?

JOHN   True. (*Chuckles*) You wouldn't believe how nervous I was. And she didn't make it any easier . . .
Pretended the whole thing was a complete surprise.
Bernhardt couldn't have done it nicer . . . Or looked
nicer . . . All in blue . . . Blue dress, blue hat, blue
shoes . . . Everything blue . . . Light blue . . . And
dignified . . . One look at her, you knew she was a
lady . . . My family *called* her The Lady. To their
minds it was an insult. (*Regards* TIMMY) How did we
get on this?

TIMMY   You were—
          (*He is interrupted by the opening of the outside
          door.* NETTIE *enters*)

JOHN   Join the party.
          (*She enters the kitchen*)

TIMMY   We're having a little hair of the dog.

NETTIE   How was the game?

JOHN   One-sided.

TIMMY   Pop was just telling me how you and he met.
          (NETTIE *turns to* JOHN *questioningly*)

JOHN   He asked me.

TIMMY   (*To his mother, indicating his father*)   His version is a little different from yours.

NETTIE   What do you mean?

TIMMY   He says *you* chased *him.*

NETTIE   That'll be the day.

TIMMY   Says you did everything but stand on your head

to attract his attention. (NETTIE *is not sure now whether he's kidding or not*) That's what he said.

(NETTIE *looks uncertainly from* TIMMY *to* JOHN. *They break up simultaneously*)

NETTIE You two.

JOHN How about a beer?

NETTIE No thanks.

JOHN Come on—

TIMMY Be a sport.

NETTIE All right.

JOHN That-a-girl.

NETTIE Just a glass. (*To* TIMMY, *while* JOHN *gets the beer*) What *did* he tell you?

TIMMY He said you were dressed in blue and nobody ever looked nicer.

NETTIE I'll bet.

TIMMY (*To* JOHN) Didn't you say that?

JOHN I'm a stranger here.

NETTIE Did he tell you how he used his friend Eddie Barnes?

JOHN Bless us and save us.

NETTIE Every night they'd get on the subway, stand right in front of me, and have a loud conversation about how well they were doing in business.

JOHN It wasn't every night.

NETTIE Poor Eddie had to go an hour out of his way.

TIMMY That's what I call a friend.

JOHN The best I ever had. (*Extends a glass of beer to* NETTIE) Here you go. (*She stares past him*) Here's your beer.
> (*She continues looking off. He follows her gaze to the roses*)

NETTIE Where did they come from?

TIMMY Pop got them . . . for you.

NETTIE (*To* JOHN) You did?

JOHN Yes.
> (*She goes to the roses*)

NETTIE They're beautiful . . . Thank you.

JOHN You're welcome.

NETTIE What made you do it?

JOHN We happened to pass a place and I know you like them.

NETTIE I haven't had red roses since Papa died. (*To* TIMMY) He used to send me a dozen on my birthday. Never missed.

TIMMY I remember.

NETTIE (*To* JOHN) Thank you.

JOHN You're welcome.

NETTIE I'm going to cry.
> (*She does*)

JOHN You don't bring flowers—they cry. You do—they cry.

NETTIE I'm sorry.

TIMMY What's to be sorry?

NETTIE He was the kindest, gentlest man that ever lived.

TIMMY I know.

NETTIE I'm all right now.

JOHN (*Handing her the glass of beer*) Here's what you need.

NETTIE Maybe so.

TIMMY (*Raising his beer*) To happy days.

JOHN and NETTIE To happy days.
    (*They all drink*)

NETTIE (*Regarding the roses*) They're just beautiful.

JOHN (*Anxious to change the subject*) Talking of Eddie Barnes before, God rest his soul, reminds me of the time old Emerson put up a second-hand car for the man who sold the most coffee over a three-month period. I won it, but couldn't drive. Eddie said he'd teach me. We didn't get two blocks from the office when he ran broadside into an ice truck.

NETTIE How about that ride to Connecticut? He practically killed us all.

JOHN What was the name of the place we stayed at?

NETTIE The Rainbow Grove.

JOHN That's right. Big fat red-haired dame ran it.

NETTIE Mrs. Hanlon.

JOHN (*Mimicking Mrs. Hanlon à la Mae West*) "My friends all call me Daisy." (*He and* NETTIE *laugh*) I dubbed her the Will Rogers of Connecticut—she never met a man she didn't like.
    (*They all laugh*)

NETTIE Remember the night you, Eddie, and a couple of

others picked her up, bed and all, and left her sleeping in the middle of the baseball field.

JOHN   In the morning when we went out to play, she was still there.

TIMMY   What did you do?

JOHN   We ruled that any ball hitting her on the fly was a ground rule double. (*They all laugh*) We had a lot of fun at that place.

NETTIE   Yes.

JOHN   I wonder if it's still there.

NETTIE   I wonder.

JOHN   Let's take a ride someday and see.

NETTIE   All right.
        (*She starts to rise*)

JOHN   Where you going?

NETTIE   Have to start supper.

JOHN   Forget it—we're eating out!

NETTIE   I bought a steak.

JOHN   It'll keep. (*To* TIMMY) Where would you like to go, Champ?

NETTIE   Maybe he has a date.

JOHN   Bring her along.

TIMMY   I don't have a date.

NETTIE   I thought you'd be seeing that Davis girl?

TIMMY   That's finished.

NETTIE   She was a nice girl.

155

JOHN She was a dunce.

NETTIE John!

TIMMY Pop's right.

NETTIE You men are terrible.

TIMMY You're too kind.

JOHN Well, where are we going?

TIMMY You two settle it while I see a man about a dog. (*He exits*)

JOHN How about the Concourse Plaza?

NETTIE All right.

JOHN I had a nice day today.

NETTIE I'm glad.

JOHN He's quite a boy.

NETTIE That's what I've been telling you for years.

JOHN We talked about things. Really talked. The way Eddie and I used to . . . The hell with the Concourse Plaza! Let's go downtown! Let's go to the New Yorker!

NETTIE You *are* in a good mood.

JOHN Because I want to go downtown?

NETTIE That and the roses.

JOHN Are you going to talk about those roses all night?

NETTIE I just wanted to thank you for them.

JOHN You already have.

NETTIE You sound as though you're sorry you got them.

JOHN Don't be ridiculous.

NETTIE   Then what are you angry about?

JOHN   I'm just tired of hearing about them. A guy gets some roses—big deal.

NETTIE   You're embarrassed.

JOHN   I am not.

NETTIE   You did something nice and you're embarrassed.

JOHN   You don't know what you're talking about.

NETTIE   Don't worry, I won't tell anyone.

JOHN   *Nettie, please.*

NETTIE   All right, but I want to let you know how much I appreciate it.

JOHN   Good. I'm glad.

NETTIE   I do . . . I really do. (*On an impulse she touches his shoulder. The contact is mutually startling. Flustered, she turns away*) We haven't been to the New Yorker in years . . . I wonder if they still have the ice show? . . . Do you suppose we'll have any trouble getting in on a Saturday night?
   (TIMMY *enters*)

TIMMY   What did you decide?

JOHN   We're going to the Hotel New Yorker.

TIMMY   Well, digga digga doo.

JOHN   After that we're going to the Diamond Horseshoe. And then the Sawdust Trail.

TIMMY   Sounds like our night to howl.

JOHN   That's what it is.
   (*He howls*)

157

TIMMY   You call that a howl?
(*He howls louder. Now* JOHN *howls. Now* TIMMY.
Now JOHN. *Now* TIMMY. *Each howl is louder than
the last*)
                    Curtain

Scene 3

Time: Two A.M. *Sunday morning.*

At rise: The apartment is in darkness. From the hallway outside the apartment, we hear TIMMY *and* JOHN *in loud but dubious harmony.*

TIMMY *and* JOHN (*Offstage*) "Farewell, Piccadilly . . . Hello, Leicester Square . . . It's a long, long way to Tipperary . . . But my heart's right there."

NETTIE (*Offstage*) You'll wake the Feldmans.

JOHN (*Offstage*) Nothing could wake the Feldmans.
      (TIMMY *and* JOHN *laugh*)

NETTIE (*Offstage*) Open the door.

JOHN (*Offstage*) Can't find my keys.

TIMMY (*Offstage—giggling*) I can't find the door.

NETTIE (*Offstage*) Honestly.

JOHN (*Offstage*) Where would you be if you were my keys?

NETTIE (*Offstage*) Here—I'll do it.

JOHN (*Offstage*) Did you ever see such pretty hair?

NETTIE (*Offstage*) Stop.

TIMMY (*Offstage*) Beautiful hair.

NETTIE (*Offstage*) Will you please let me open this door?
      (*A key turns. The door opens.* NETTIE, *followed by* JOHN *and* TIMMY, *enters. She turns on the lights*)

JOHN   Home to wife and mother.

NETTIE   (*To* JOHN)   Someday we'll break our necks because you refuse to leave a light.

TIMMY   (*Sings*)   "By the light . . . (JOHN *joins in*) Of the silvery moon—"

NETTIE   That's just enough.

JOHN   Whatever you say, Antoinette.

NETTIE   I say to bed.

JOHN   Shank of the evening. (*He grabs her around the waist and manages a squeeze before she breaks away. Ignoring the look of censure she directs at him, he turns to* TIMMY) No sir, you can't beat a law degree. Springboard for anything.

TIMMY   So they say.

NETTIE   (*To* JOHN)   Anyone can be a lawyer. How many people become writers?

JOHN   That's my point.

NETTIE   You should be proud to have a son who wants to try something different.

JOHN   Did I say I wasn't proud of him?

TIMMY   Abra ka dabra ka deedra slatter-in. (*They regard him*) The fellow in the red jacket who leads the horses to the post at Jamaica always says that when they reach the starting gate. Abra ka dabra ka deedra slatter-in. And here are your horses for the fifth race . . . Long as you can say it, you're not drunk . . . *Abra ka dabra ka deedra slatter-in.*

JOHN   Abra ka dabra . . .

TIMMY   Ka deedra slatter-in.

NETTIE   Honestly.

JOHN   Ka zebra—

TIMMY   Not zebra. Deedra . . . Ka deedra slatter-in . . .
Abra ka dabra ka deedra slatter-in.

JOHN   Abra . . . ka dabra . . . ka deedra . . . slatter-in.

TIMMY   Faster.

JOHN   Abra, ka dabra, ka deedra, slatter-in.

TIMMY   Faster.

JOHN   Abra ka dabra ka deedra slatter-in.

NETTIE   Have you both lost your minds?

JOHN   Nothing wrong with us that a little nightcap
wouldn't cure.
    (*He enters the kitchen*)

NETTIE   (*Following him*)   I'll nightcap you.

TIMMY   I can't bear to hear married people fight.

JOHN   (*To* NETTIE)   We ought to go dancing more.

NETTIE   Now I know you're drunk.

TIMMY   (*Calling from the living room*)   Who was it that
used to call us The Four Mortons?

JOHN   (*Calling back*)   Harold Bowen.

TIMMY   (*Staring at the audience*)   I wish we were.

JOHN   (*To* NETTIE)   Remember the first dance I took you
to?

NETTIE   Of course.

JOHN   I'll bet you don't.

NETTIE Of course I do.

TIMMY (*Lost in contemplation of the audience*) I have
this magical feeling about vaudeville.

JOHN (*To* NETTIE) Where was it, then?

NETTIE The Crystal Terrace.

JOHN And what was the first song?

NETTIE It's too late for quiz games.

TIMMY It doesn't matter how cheap and tinny the show
is . . . Soon as the house lights go down and the band
starts up, I could cry.

JOHN (*To* NETTIE) The first song we ever danced to was
"Pretty Baby." A blond guy crooned it.

NETTIE Through a gold megaphone.

JOHN You *do* remember.

NETTIE Of course.
(JOHN *moves to touch* NETTIE. *To elude him, she
re-enters the living room. He follows*)

TIMMY (*To the audience—à la Smith and Dale*) "I've
got snew in my blood" . . . "What's snew?" . . . "Nothing. What's snew with you?"

NETTIE (*To* JOHN—*indicating* TIMMY) What's he doing?

JOHN Playing the Palace.

TIMMY (*To the audience*) "Take off the coat, my boy
. . . Take . . . off . . . the . . . coat . . . Tay-ake . . .
o-f-f-f-f . . . the coat-t-t-t-t."

JOHN and TIMMY "The coat is off."

NETTIE (*To* TIMMY) Will you please go to bed?

162

TIMMY (*To the audience*)   In closing I would like to do a dance made famous by the inimitable Pat Rooney. (*Nods to* JOHN) Maestro, if you please.
> (JOHN *begins to hum "The Daughter of Rosie O'Grady" as both he and* TIMMY *dance in the manner of Pat Rooney*)

NETTIE   John! Timmy! (*They stop dancing*) Mama expects us at twelve.

TIMMY (*To the audience*)   We're running a bit long, folks: No dance tonight. My mother thanks you. My father thanks you. My sister thanks you. And the Feldmans thank you. (*He goes into Jimmy Durante's closing song*) "Good night . . . Good night . . . Good night—"

NETTIE   *Good night.*

TIMMY (*Kisses* NETTIE)   Good night, Mrs. Cleary—whoever you are.

NETTIE   Good night, dear.

TIMMY (*To* JOHN—*indicating the audience*)   Tough house, but I warmed them up for you.

JOHN   Thanks.

TIMMY   Don't look now, but your leg's broken.

JOHN   The show must go on.

TIMMY (*To* NETTIE—*indicating* JOHN)   Plucky lad. (*Extends his hand to* JOHN) Honor to share the bill with you.

JOHN (*Shaking with him*)   Likewise.

TIMMY   Sleep well, chaps.

JOHN   Night, Champ.

NETTIE Sure you don't want an Alka Seltzer?

TIMMY Abra ka dabra ka deedra slatter-in . . . see you in the morning.

JOHN With the help of God.

TIMMY (*Moving toward his room*) Abra ka dabra ka deedra slatter-in . . . Abra ka dabra ka deedra slatter-in . . . And here are your horses for . . .
(*He enters his room, closes the door*)

NETTIE Home two days and both nights to bed like that.

JOHN He's entitled. You should hear some of the things he's been through. They overran one of those concentration camps—

NETTIE I don't want to hear about it now.

JOHN You're right. It's no way to end a happy evening.

NETTIE I think we have some aspirin in the kitchen.
(*She moves into the kitchen. He follows, watches her take a bottle of aspirin from a cabinet*)

JOHN You didn't say anything before about a headache.

NETTIE I don't have a headache.

JOHN Then what—

NETTIE I read that if you put an aspirin in cut flowers they keep longer. (*She drops an aspirin in the vase, regards the roses*) I wonder what made you get them?

JOHN I don't know.

NETTIE There must have been some reason.

JOHN I just thought it would be nice to do.
(*She turns to him*)

NETTIE   It was.
   (*They regard each other a moment*)

JOHN   I like your dress.

NETTIE   You've seen it before.

JOHN   It looks different . . . Everything about you looks different.

NETTIE   What Mass are you going to?

JOHN   Ten o'clock.

NETTIE (*Picking up the vase of roses and starting toward the living room.*)   I better set the alarm.

JOHN   Nettie? (*She turns to him*) I had a good time tonight.

NETTIE   So did I.
   (NETTIE *enters the living room and places the roses on a table*)

JOHN (*Following her into the living room*)   Did you really? Or were you putting it on for his sake?

NETTIE   I really did.

JOHN   So did I.

NETTIE   I'll set the alarm for nine-fifteen.
   (*She starts away again*)

JOHN   Now that he's back we'll have lots of good times.
   (*She stops*)

NETTIE   What's wrong between you and I has nothing to do with him.

JOHN   I didn't say it did.

NETTIE   We have to solve our own problems.

JOHN (*Coming up behind her*) Of course.

NETTIE They can't be solved in one night.

JOHN (*Touching her*) I know.

NETTIE One nice evening doesn't make everything different.

JOHN Did I say it did?
(*His lips brush the nape of her neck*)

NETTIE I guess you don't understand.

JOHN I forgot how nice you smelled.

NETTIE You'll spoil everything.

JOHN I want things right between us.

NETTIE You think this is going to make them right?

JOHN (*His hand moving to her breasts*) We have to start some place.

NETTIE (*Breaking away*) Start?

JOHN Bless us and save us.

NETTIE *That's not my idea of a start.*

JOHN Nettie, I want you . . . I want you like I never wanted anything in my life.

NETTIE (*Covering her ears*) Stop.

JOHN *Please?*

NETTIE You're drunk.

JOHN *Do you think I could ask again if I wasn't?*

NETTIE I'm not one of your hotel lobby whores.

JOHN If you were I wouldn't have to ask.

NETTIE A couple of drinks, a couple of jokes, and let's jump in bed.

JOHN Maybe that's my mistake.

NETTIE How do you suppose Ruskin managed without you today?

JOHN Maybe you don't want to be asked!
    (*He seizes her*)

NETTIE Let me alone.

JOHN (*As they struggle*) You've had the drinks! You've had the jokes!

NETTIE *Stop!*
    (*She breaks free of him; regards him for a moment, then picks up the vase of roses and hurls them against the floor. The impact is shattering. They both freeze. For a moment there is silence. Now* TIMMY's *door opens*)

TIMMY (*Entering*) What happened?

NETTIE The roses . . . I knocked them over.

TIMMY Sounded like a bomb.

NETTIE I'm sorry I woke you. (TIMMY *bends to pick up a piece of the vase*) Don't . . . I'll clean up. You go back to bed. (*He hesitates*) Please.

TIMMY All right . . . Good night.

NETTIE Good night.

TIMMY Good night, Pop.
    (JOHN, *his back to* TIMMY, *remains silent.* TIMMY *hesitates a moment, then goes off to his room and closes his door*)

NETTIE (*To* JOHN) You moved me this afternoon . . . When you brought the roses, I felt something stir I thought was dead forever. (*Regards the roses on the floor*) And now this . . . I don't understand.

JOHN (*Without turning*) I had nothing to do with the roses . . . They were *his* idea.
(*She bends and starts to pick up the roses*)
Curtain

Act Two

Scene 1

Time: Nine-fifteen A.M. *Sunday morning.*

At rise: JOHN *and* NETTIE *are at the breakfast table.*

JOHN Coffee's weak.

NETTIE Add water.

JOHN I said *weak* . . . Waste of time bringing good coffee into this house . . . (*He looks for a reaction. She offers none*) I'm thinking about renting the lake house this summer . . . (*Still no reaction from her*) Business is off . . . (*Still no reaction*) Well, what do you say?

NETTIE About what?

JOHN Renting the lake house.

NETTIE Timmy will be disappointed.

JOHN How about you?

NETTIE I'm in favor of it.

JOHN Of course you are.

NETTIE I wonder why.
(TIMMY *enters*)

TIMMY Morning.

NETTIE Good morning.
(TIMMY *kisses her*)

TIMMY (*To* JOHN) Morning.

JOHN Nice of you to join us.

TIMMY My pleasure.

JOHN   This isn't a hotel. We have our meals at certain times.

(TIMMY *now senses his father's irritation*)

TIMMY   You should have woke me.

NETTIE (*To* TIMMY)   It's all right.

JOHN   Of course it is.

NETTIE (*To* TIMMY, *who regards his father puzzledly*) Sit down. (TIMMY *sits*) What do you want?

TIMMY   Coffee.

NETTIE   Just coffee?

TIMMY   Stomach's a bit shaky.

NETTIE   You should have taken that Alka Seltzer.

TIMMY   I'll be all right.

JOHN   Two days—two hangovers. Is that what they taught you in the army?

TIMMY (*To* JOHN)   Cream, please? (JOHN *passes the cream*) Thank you.

JOHN   I'm thinking of renting the lake house.

TIMMY   How come?

JOHN   I can use the money.

TIMMY   Oh . . .

JOHN   That all you're going to say?

TIMMY   What do you expect me to say?

JOHN   I thought that house meant something to you.

TIMMY   It does. But if you need the money—

JOHN   A bunch of strangers sleeping in our beds, using our things—doesn't bother you at all?

TIMMY   If it has to be it has to be.

JOHN   Of course! I forgot! What's a little summer cottage, after the earth-shattering things you've been through?

TIMMY   (*To* NETTIE—*holding up the cream pitcher*)   Do you have more cream?

NETTIE   (*Taking the pitcher*)   Yes.

JOHN   What do you want more cream for?

TIMMY   Coffee's strong.

JOHN   It's weak.

TIMMY   It's too strong for me. (NETTIE *returns the refilled pitcher to him*) Thanks.
   (*He adds cream to his coffee*)

JOHN   A few months in the army and they're experts on everything. Even coffee.

TIMMY   Who said that?

JOHN   By the time I was your age I was in the coffee business nine years . . . Nine years . . . When I was seventeen they sent me to Brazil for three months.

TIMMY   I know.

JOHN   I'd never even been out of New York before but I went down there on my own and did my job.

TIMMY   For Emerson, wasn't it?

JOHN   No uniform. No buddies. No Uncle Sam to lean on. Just myself . . . All alone in that strange place.

TIMMY   That's the time you grew the mustache to look older.

JOHN Who's telling the story?

TIMMY Sorry.

JOHN Thirty-five years in the business and *he's* going to tell me about coffee.

TIMMY I wasn't telling you anything about anything. I just said that for me, the coffee was too strong.

JOHN It isn't strong!

TIMMY (*To* NETTIE) What time's dinner?

NETTIE Mama expects us at twelve.

JOHN I suppose you'll wear your uniform.

TIMMY It's the only thing I have that fits.

JOHN Are you sure? I mean maybe you haven't grown as much as you think.
(TIMMY, *studiously trying to avoid a fight, turns to* NETTIE)

TIMMY Ravioli?

NETTIE And meat balls.

JOHN G.I. Bill, home loans, discharge bonus, unemployment insurance—you boys did pretty well for yourselves.

NETTIE They did pretty well for us, too.

JOHN (*Sings*) "Oh, say can you see."

TIMMY What's your point, Pop?

JOHN The war's over.

TIMMY I'll buy that.

JOHN The world doesn't owe anyone a living—including veterans.

TIMMY   I'll buy that too.

JOHN   Let the Jews support you.

TIMMY   Come again?

JOHN   Wasn't for them we wouldn't have gotten in it in the first place.

TIMMY   I thought you broke that record.

JOHN   Lousy kikes.

NETTIE   John!

TIMMY   (*To* NETTIE)   I changed my mind—I'll have some toast.

JOHN   (*To* TIMMY)   Don't tell me you've lost your great love for the Jews?

NETTIE   *Stop it!*

TIMMY   (*To* NETTIE)   It's all right.

JOHN   How nice of you to let me talk in my own house. And me not even a veteran.

TIMMY   Would you mind telling me what you're mad about?

JOHN   Who's mad?

NETTIE   (*To* TIMMY)   Anything on the toast?

TIMMY   Honey, if you've got it.

JOHN   A man states a few facts and right away he's mad.

NETTIE   (*At the cupboard*)   How about strawberry jam?

TIMMY   No.

JOHN   If I get a halfway decent offer I might sell the lake house.

NETTIE Peach?

TIMMY All right.

JOHN Hurry up with your breakfast.

TIMMY What for?

JOHN Mass starts in twenty minutes and you're not even dressed.

TIMMY Mass?

JOHN Mass.

TIMMY I haven't been to Mass in over two years. You know that.

JOHN Lots of bad habits you boys picked up that you'll have to get over.

TIMMY Not going to Mass isn't a habit I picked up. It's a decision I came to after a lot of thought.

JOHN What way is that for a Catholic to talk?

TIMMY I haven't considered myself a Catholic for quite a while.

JOHN Must be something wrong with my ears.

NETTIE (To JOHN) You knew this was coming. Why pretend it's such a shock?

JOHN Now there's a familiar alliance. (To TIMMY) So you've outgrown the Faith?

TIMMY It doesn't answer my needs.

JOHN Outgrown your old clothes and outgrown the Faith.

TIMMY Pop, will you listen to me—

JOHN Billions of people have believed in it since the beginning of time but it's not good enough for you.

TIMMY It's not a question of good enough.

JOHN What do you say when people ask what religion you are?

TIMMY Nothing.

JOHN You say you're nothing?

TIMMY Yes.

JOHN The Clearys have been Catholics since . . . since the beginning of time. And now you, a Cleary, are going to tell people that you're nothing?

TIMMY Yes.

JOHN *You're an atheist!*

NETTIE John!

JOHN When you come to the blank after religion on those college applications, put down atheist. Make a big hit in those Ivy League places, from what I hear.

TIMMY I'm not an atheist.

JOHN Then what are you?

TIMMY I don't know . . . But I'd like a chance to find out.

JOHN You don't know what you believe in?

TIMMY Do *you?*

JOHN Yes.

TIMMY Tell me . . . Well, go on!

JOHN I believe in the Father, the Son and the Holy Ghost . . . I believe that God created man in his own image . . . I—

TIMMY   Pop, look . . . if your faith works for you, I'm glad. I'm very glad. I wish it worked for me . . . But it doesn't.

JOHN   Do you believe in God—yes or no?

TIMMY   I don't believe in Heaven, or Hell, or Purgatory, or—

JOHN   *Yes or no?*

TIMMY   I believe there's something bigger than myself. What you call it or what it is I don't know.

JOHN   Well, this is a fine how-do-you-do.

NETTIE   (*To* JOHN)   Yesterday you said he was a man. A man has a right to decide such things for himself.

JOHN   "Good morning, Father Riley." "Good morning, Mr. Cleary. I understand your boy's out of service." "Yes, Father." "Where is he this fine Sunday morning, Mr. Cleary?" "Home, Father." "Is he sick, Mr. Cleary?" "No, Father." "Then why isn't he here in church, Mr. Cleary?" "He's become an atheist, Father."

TIMMY   I'm not an atheist!

JOHN   Whatever you are, I won't have it! I'm the boss of this house. If you want to go on living here you'll do as I say. And I say you're going to church with me this morning.

NETTIE   (*To* JOHN)   *Do you know what you're doing?*

JOHN   (*To* NETTIE)   Keep out! (*To* TIMMY) Well?

NETTIE   (*To* TIMMY)   Don't pay any attention to him.

TIMMY   (*To* NETTIE)   It's all right. (*To* JOHN) I'll go to church with you. (*Rises*) Be out in a minute.
       (*He starts from the room*)

JOHN   Forget it!

TIMMY   What?

JOHN   I said forget it. The Lord doesn't want anybody in His house who has to be dragged there. (*To* NETTIE *as he puts on his jacket*) Score another one for your side.

TIMMY   It has nothing to do with her.

JOHN   (*To* TIMMY) Wait till you're down on all fours someday—you'll be glad to see a priest then.
     (*He starts out*)

NETTIE   We'll meet you at Mama's.

JOHN   I won't be there.

NETTIE   She expects us.

JOHN   We all have our disappointments.

TIMMY   I said I'd go with you.
     (JOHN *exits, slamming the door*)

NETTIE   Now what was that all about?

TIMMY   (*Furious with himself*)   I should have gone with him.

NETTIE   I'll never understand that man.

TIMMY   Why didn't I just go? Why did I have to make an issue?

NETTIE   It wasn't your fault.

TIMMY   It never *is*.

NETTIE   When he's in one of those moods there's nothing anyone can do.

TIMMY   The alliance, he called us.

NETTIE   Everyone's entitled to their own beliefs.

TIMMY   That's what we must seem like to him—an alliance. Always two against one. Always us against him . . . Why?

NETTIE   If you're through eating, I'll clear the table.

TIMMY   Didn't you hear me?

NETTIE   Evidently your father's not the only one who got up on the wrong side of the bed this morning.

TIMMY   *I'm not talking about this morning.*

NETTIE   There's no need to shout.

TIMMY   You, and him, and me, and what's been going on here for twenty years . . . It's got to stop.

NETTIE   What's got to stop?

TIMMY   *We've* got to stop ganging up on him.

NETTIE   Is that what we've been doing?

TIMMY   You said you've never understood him.

NETTIE   And never will.

TIMMY   Have you ever really tried? . . .

NETTIE   Go on.

TIMMY   Have you ever tried to see things from his point of view?

NETTIE   What things?

TIMMY   The lake house, for instance.

NETTIE   The lake house?

TIMMY   It's the pride and joy of his life and you're always knocking it.

NETTIE   Do you know why?

TIMMY   Because he bought it without consulting you.

NETTIE   Drove me out to this Godforsaken lake. Pointed to a bungalow with no heat or hot water and said, "That's where we'll be spending our summers from now on."

TIMMY   An hour's ride from New York City isn't exactly Godforsaken.

NETTIE   It wasn't an hour's ride twenty years ago.

TIMMY   The point is, would he have gotten it any other way? If he had come to you and said he wanted to buy a cottage on a lake in New Jersey, would you have said yes?

NETTIE   I might have.

TIMMY   No. Not if it had been a palace with fifty servants.

NETTIE   I don't like the country.

TIMMY   We'd have spent every summer right here.

NETTIE   My idea of a vacation is to travel—see something new.

TIMMY   You had a chance to see Brazil.

NETTIE   That was different.

TIMMY   The fellow who took that job is a millionaire today.

NETTIE   And still living in Brazil.

TIMMY   Which is not to be compared with the Bronx.

NETTIE   So it's my fault we're not millionaires.

TIMMY   Who knows—your mother might have loved Brazil! (*This causes her to turn from him*) You violently objected to moving from Yorkville to the Bronx . . . Why?

NETTIE (*Clearing the table in an effort to avoid him*) I hate the Bronx.

TIMMY (*Pursuing her*) But you insisted that your mother move up here.

NETTIE They tore down her building. She had to move somewhere.

TIMMY Except for summers at the lake, have you ever gone two days without seeing her?

NETTIE Only because of Willis. (*He starts from the room*) Where are you going?

TIMMY To get dressed. Then I'm going to church and apologize to him for acting like a fool.

NETTIE You'll be at Mama's for dinner?

TIMMY Only if he'll come with me.

NETTIE You disappointed Willis yesterday. You can't do it again.

TIMMY Oh yes I can!

NETTIE How cruel.

TIMMY Not as cruel as your dragging me over there every day when I was little. And when I was bigger, and couldn't go every day, concentrating on Sunday. "Is it too much to give your crippled cousin one day a week?" And when I didn't go there on Sunday, I felt so guilty that I couldn't enjoy myself anyway . . . I hate Sunday, and I don't think I'll ever get over it. But I'm going to try.

NETTIE   How fortunate for the cripples in this world that everyone isn't as selfish as you.

TIMMY   Why do you keep calling him a cripple? That's not the worst thing wrong with Willis. It's his mind. He's like a four-year-old.

NETTIE   Can a four-year-old read a book?

TIMMY   (*Pressing his attack relentlessly*)   Yes, he reads. After you drilling him every day for twenty years. But does he have any idea what he's reading about? . . . If you and the rest of them over there want to throw your lives away on him, you go ahead and do it! But don't try and sacrifice me to the cause! (NETTIE, *stunned by* TIMMY's *assault, exits from the kitchen, disappears into the bedroom. Immediately regretful at having vented his feelings so strongly,* TIMMY *moves into the living room; is pondering the best way to apologize, when* NETTIE, *carrying a pocketbook, appears, takes a coat from the hall closet, puts it on*) Where are you going? (*No answer*) Your mother doesn't expect us till twelve. (*No answer*) Give me a minute to dress and I'll go with you. (*No answer*) Now look—(*As* NETTIE *reaches for her pocketbook,* TIMMY *also reaches for it in an effort to prevent her departure. He wrests it from her. As he does so, his face registers surprise*) This is like lead. (*He opens the bag, regards the contents, looks at her puzzledly*) You've got all your coins in here . . . You're taking your coins . . . What for? (*She extends her hand for the bag. He surrenders it. She moves toward the door*) Will you please say something?

NETTIE   Thank you for the roses.
    (*She exits*)
             Curtain

Scene 2

Time: Ten P.M. *Sunday.*

At rise: TIMMY, *highball glass in hand, whiskey bottle on the coffee table before him, sits on the sofa in the living room. It is plain that he has been drinking for some time.* JOHN, *cold sober, moves about the room nervously.*

TIMMY I remember sitting here like this the night she went to have John.

JOHN Why would she just walk out and not tell anyone where she was going?

TIMMY I was six.

JOHN Without any reason.

TIMMY Dr. Goldman came at midnight and took her to the hospital.

JOHN It doesn't make sense.

TIMMY After they left, I started to cry. You did too.

JOHN It's not like her.

TIMMY I asked you if you loved her. You nodded. I asked you to say it. You hesitated. I got hysterical. To quiet me you finally said, "I love her."

JOHN Maybe she's at Sophie's.

TIMMY No. (JOHN *regards him questioningly*) I called Sophie.

JOHN (*Looking at a pocket watch*) It's after ten.

TIMMY I called everybody.

184

JOHN She's been gone twelve hours.

TIMMY They all said they'd call back if they heard from her.

JOHN If she's not here by eleven o'clock I'm calling the police.

TIMMY I wonder what difference it would have made if John lived.

JOHN I wonder what department you call.

TIMMY I remember you and I going to visit her at the hospital on a Sunday afternoon. I had to wait downstairs. First time I ever heard the word incubator . . . In-cubator.

JOHN I guess you call Missing Persons.

TIMMY As we left the hospital and started down the Concourse, we ran into an exotic Spanish-looking woman whom you'd met on one of your trips to Brazil. She was a dancer. Very beautiful. You and she spoke awhile and then you and I went to a movie. Fred Astaire and Ginger Rogers in *Flying Down to Rio*.

JOHN What are you talking about?

TIMMY I always thought that was a coincidence—meeting a South American woman and then seeing a picture about Rio . . . *Was* it a coincidence?

JOHN What?

TIMMY (*Sings*) "Hey Rio, Rio by the sea-o. Got to get to Rio and I've got to make time."

JOHN You're drunk.

TIMMY Abra ka dabra ka deedra slatter-in.

JOHN   Fine time you picked for it.

TIMMY   A bunch of chorus girls stood on the wings of a silver plane singing that song—"Hey Rio. Flying down to Rio—"

JOHN   You're the last one who saw her. The police will want to question you.

TIMMY   She left the house at ten A.M., your Honor. Didn't say boo but I assumed she was going to her mother's. Brown coat. Brown hat. When I got to her mother's, she wasn't there. They hadn't seen her—hadn't heard from her. I had two helpings of ravioli and meat balls. Came back here to wait. When she didn't call by three o'clock I started to worry—

JOHN   And drink.

TIMMY   *When she didn't call by three o'clock I started to worry* . . . I tried to get in touch with my father. Called all the bars I could think of—"Is Mr. Cleary there?" . . . "If he comes in would you please tell him to call his house?" . . . It was like old times.

JOHN   I told you—I had dinner and went to a movie.

TIMMY   "*Is* Mr. Cleary there?"—Shows how long I've been away. You never say, "*Is* Mr. Cleary there?" You say, "Let me speak to Mr. Cleary." As though you *knew* he was there.

JOHN   I was at a movie.

TIMMY   Did it have a happy ending?

JOHN   *Gilda,* with Rita Hayworth and Glenn Ford.

TIMMY   I didn't ask you what it was.

JOHN   At the Loew's Paradise.

TIMMY   *I didn't ask you what it was!*

JOHN   What's the matter with you?

TIMMY   (*About to pour another drink*)   Join me?

JOHN   No, and I think you've had enough.

TIMMY   First time I ever saw you refuse a drink.

JOHN   I want you to stop.

TIMMY   But you're powerless to stop me. It's a lousy position to be in, *I* know.

JOHN   That's your last one.
(*He starts to remove the bottle*)

TIMMY   Take it and I leave!
(JOHN *hesitates, puts the bottle down*)

JOHN   Joy, joy, said Mrs. Malloy.

TIMMY   Louder louder, said Mrs. . . . What rhymes with louder?

JOHN   You were sick Friday night. Sick last night.
(*The phone rings. By the time* TIMMY *gets to his feet* JOHN *is picking up the receiver*)

JOHN (*On the phone*)   Hello? . . . Oh . . . (*The abrupt disinterest in his voice causes* TIMMY *to sit down*) Nothing . . . I said we haven't heard anything . . . I know how long she's been gone . . . Of course I'm concerned . . . *I don't care how I sound—I'm concerned* . . . If she's not here by eleven, that's what I'm going to do . . . That's a comforting bit of information. (*He hangs up, returns to the living room*) Her mother again. Wanted to let me know how many muggings there's been lately.

TIMMY   I've got it! Earl Browder.

JOHN What?

TIMMY Louder, louder, said Mrs. Earl Browder.

JOHN I'm glad you can take the whole thing so calmly.

TIMMY To quote a famous authority: "I don't care how I sound—I'm concerned."

JOHN (*Regards his watch*) Ten after ten.

TIMMY Trouble with you is you haven't had enough experience in these matters.

JOHN Where the devil can she be?

TIMMY I'm an old hand.

JOHN Never done anything like this before in her life.

TIMMY All those nights I lay in bed waiting for your key to turn in the door. Part of me praying you'd come home safe, part of me dreading the sound of that key because I knew there'd be a fight.

JOHN I'll give her a few minutes more.

TIMMY All those mornings I woke up sick. Had to miss school. The boy's delicate, everyone said, has a weak constitution.

JOHN I'll give her till half-past.

TIMMY From the day I left this house I was never sick. Not once. Took me a long time to see the connection.

JOHN Where can she go? She has no money.

TIMMY Wrong.

JOHN What?

TIMMY Nothing.

JOHN You said wrong.

TIMMY (*Sings*) "Hey Rio. Rio by the—"

JOHN I want to know what you meant.

TIMMY She took her coins. (JOHN *goes into the bedroom*)

TIMMY (*Quietly*) "Hey Rio. Rio by the sea-o."
   (JOHN *reappears*)

JOHN Why didn't you mention it before?

TIMMY Slipped my mind.

JOHN Over fifty dollars in dimes and quarters, and she took them all.

TIMMY Person could go quite a ways with fifty dollars.

JOHN You saw her take them?

TIMMY Yes.

JOHN Didn't it strike you as peculiar?

TIMMY Everything strikes me as peculiar.

JOHN There's something you're not telling me.

TIMMY We all have our little secrets.

JOHN There *is* something!

TIMMY Take you and your money for instance.

JOHN I want to know what it is.

TIMMY For all I know, we're millionaires.

JOHN I want to know why she walked out.

TIMMY Just between us chickens, how much do you have?
   (TIMMY *reaches for the bottle to pour another drink, but* JOHN *snatches it out of his reach*)

JOHN Answer me.

TIMMY If you don't put that bottle down, I'm leaving.

JOHN I want an answer!

TIMMY (*Rising*) See you around the pool hall.

JOHN (*Shoving him down hard on the sofa*) *I want an answer!*

TIMMY Hell of a way to treat a veteran.

JOHN I've taken all the crap from you I'm going to.

TIMMY You want an answer. I want a drink. It's a deal. (*He reaches for the bottle but* JOHN *keeps it from him*)

JOHN First the answer.

TIMMY I forget the question.

JOHN Why did your mother leave this house? . . . Well?

TIMMY We had an argument.

JOHN About what?

TIMMY I don't remember.

JOHN Probably something to do with your drinking.

TIMMY Yes, that's what it was. She said I drank too much.

JOHN She's right.

TIMMY Yes.

JOHN I never thought I'd see the day when you and she would argue.

TIMMY Neither did I.

JOHN She didn't say where she was going? Just took the coins and left?

TIMMY That's right.

JOHN Beats me.
(*He starts toward the kitchen*)

TIMMY Where you going?

JOHN To get something to eat.

TIMMY *Eat?*

JOHN I didn't have any supper.

TIMMY A minute ago you were so worried you couldn't even sit down.

JOHN I'm just going to have a sandwich.

TIMMY Have a banquet!

JOHN What are you getting mad at *me* for? You're the one who argued with her.

TIMMY Which absolves you completely! She might jump off a bridge but *your* conscience is clear!

JOHN A person doesn't take a bunch of change along if they're planning to do something like that.

TIMMY *She thanked me for the roses!* (JOHN *just looks at him*) Don't you have any consideration for other people's feelings?

JOHN Consideration?

TIMMY Don't you know how much it pleased her to think they were from you?

JOHN *You* talk about consideration?

TIMMY How could you do it?

JOHN Do you have any idea how I looked forward to this morning? To Mass, and dropping in at Rafferty's afterwards with you in your uniform?

TIMMY Always the injured party.

JOHN You'll be the injured party in about two minutes.

TIMMY I already am.

JOHN Real rough you had it. Good food. Good clothes. Always a roof over your head.

TIMMY Heigh-ho, everybody, it's count-your-blessings time.

JOHN I'll tell you what rough is—being so hungry you begged. Being thrown out in the street with your few sticks of furniture for all the neighbors to enjoy. Never sleeping in a bed with less than two other people. Always hiding from collectors. Having to leave school at the age of ten because your father was crippled for life and it was your job to support the house . . . You had it rough, all right.

TIMMY The subject was roses.

JOHN Where I couldn't have gone with your advantages . . . What I couldn't have been.

TIMMY I still want to know why you told her about the roses.

JOHN We were having words and it slipped out.

TIMMY Words about what? . . . Well?

JOHN Stop pushing or I'll tell you.

TIMMY Go on! Go on!

JOHN *The humping I'm getting is not worth the humping I'm getting.*

TIMMY (*Rising*) You pig.

192

JOHN   I'm warning you!

TIMMY   *You pig.* (JOHN's *right hand shoots out, catches*
TIMMY *hard across the side of his face.* NETTIE *enters)*
Bon soir. (NETTIE *regards them with an air of detached*
curiosity) Had one too many . . . Lost my ka deedra
slatter-in.

   (NETTIE *removes her hat and coat)*

JOHN   Where have you been? (NETTIE *lays her hat, coat*
and pocketbook on a chair in the foyer) I was about to
call the police. (NETTIE *gives no indication that she*
even hears him) I want to know where you've been.
(NETTIE *moves through the living room, stops in front*
of TIMMY, *who has just poured himself another drink)*
Are you going to tell me where you've been?

NETTIE   You wouldn't believe me.

JOHN   Of course I'd believe you.

NETTIE   (*To* TIMMY)   You don't look well.

TIMMY   Appearances are deceiving—I feel terrible.

JOHN   Why wouldn't I believe you?

NETTIE   You just wouldn't.

JOHN   Tell me and see.

NETTIE   I went to the movies.

JOHN   Go on.

NETTIE   That's it.

JOHN   You just went to the movies?

NETTIE   That's right.

JOHN   You've been gone over twelve hours.

NETTIE   I stayed for several shows.

JOHN   Are you trying to tell me you were at a movie for twelve hours?

NETTIE   I knew you wouldn't believe me.

TIMMY   *I* believe you.

NETTIE   Thank you.

TIMMY   What did you see?

NETTIE   That means you *don't* believe me.

TIMMY   No, I guess not.

JOHN   I demand to know where you were.

NETTIE   I went to the Hotel Astor, picked up a man, had a few drinks, a few jokes, went to his room and—

JOHN   Stop it!

NETTIE   I was just getting to the best part.

JOHN   You're making a fool of yourself.

NETTIE   Is there anything I could say that you *would* believe?

TIMMY   Say you took a bus downtown, walked around, visited a museum, had dinner, went to Radio City, and came home.

NETTIE   I took a bus downtown, walked around, visited a museum, had dinner . . .

TIMMY   Went to Radio City and came home.

NETTIE   Went to Radio City and came home.

TIMMY   I'll buy that. (*To* JOHN) If you had any sense you'd buy it, too.

JOHN I don't have any sense. I'm just a poor, ignorant slob whose wife's been missing twelve hours—and I want to know where she was.

TIMMY What difference does it make?

JOHN Stay out of this!

TIMMY How?

JOHN (*To* NETTIE) What are you going to tell your mother?

NETTIE Nothing.

JOHN The poor woman's almost out of her mind.

TIMMY There's a joke there some place.

JOHN At least call her and say you're home.

NETTIE She'll want an explanation. When I tell her, she won't believe me any more than you did.

JOHN I'll believe you when you tell the truth.

TIMMY What *is* truth? (JOHN *shoots him a furious glance*) Sorry.

NETTIE I'll tell you this . . . In all my life, the past twelve hours are the only real freedom I've ever known.

TIMMY Did you enjoy it?

NETTIE Every moment.

TIMMY Why did you come back?

NETTIE I'm a coward.

JOHN *Will somebody tell me what's going on?*

TIMMY (*To the audience*) You heard the question. (*He*

peers out into the theatre, points) Up there in the bal-
cony. The bearded gentleman with the . . . (*He stops
abruptly, rubs his stomach, regards the audience wanly*)
Sorry, folks, but I'm about to be ill.
  (*He hastens offstage.* NETTIE *follows him.* JOHN
  *takes advantage of her absence to examine her
  pocketbook, is going through it when she returns*)

NETTIE   He wouldn't let me hold his head, ordered me
out of the bathroom, locked the door.

JOHN   What happened to your coins?

NETTIE   I spent them.

JOHN   How?

NETTIE   I took a bus downtown, walked around, visited
a museum—
  (JOHN *interrupts her by slamming the pocketbook
  to the table*)

JOHN   Wasn't for his drinking, none of this would have
happened.

NETTIE   Why do you say that?

JOHN   If he didn't drink, you and he wouldn't have
argued. (*She regards him uncomprehendingly*) Isn't
that why you left? Because you had an argument about
his drinking?

NETTIE   We had an argument, but it wasn't about drinking.

JOHN   What was it about?

NETTIE   You, mostly.

JOHN   Go on.

NETTIE   He thinks I don't give you enough credit . . .
Feels you're quite a guy . . . Said we had to stop ganging up on you.
     (JOHN *turns away*)
                    Curtain

Scene 3

Time: Two A.M. Monday.

At rise: The apartment is in darkness. Now a crack of light appears beneath the door to TIMMY'S *room. The door opens.* TIMMY, *in pajamas, emerges, goes to the living room, turns on a lamp which reveals* NETTIE, *in nightgown and robe, sitting on the sofa.*

NETTIE   I couldn't sleep.

TIMMY   Neither could I. Came out to get a magazine.

NETTIE   You feel all right?

TIMMY   Yes.
   (*He looks through a pile of magazines, selects one*)

NETTIE   What time is it?

TIMMY   Almost two . . . Are *you* all right?

NETTIE   Yes.

TIMMY   Well, I guess I'll turn in. (*She offers no comment*) Good night.
   (*Again, no response. He starts away*)

NETTIE   Isn't there something you want to tell me?

TIMMY   As a matter of fact there is . . . but it'll keep till morning.

NETTIE   You've decided to leave.

TIMMY   Yes.

NETTIE   When?

TIMMY   It's not a sudden decision.

198

NETTIE When are you leaving?

TIMMY In the morning. (*He looks for a comment from her, but she remains silent*) This fellow I went to high school with has a flat on Twenty-second Street. His roommate just got married and he's looking for a replacement. I figured . . . (*He becomes aware that she isn't listening*) Hey . . . (*Still no reaction*) Hey. (*She regards him absently*) Give you a penny for them.

NETTIE An apple core.

TIMMY What?

NETTIE An apple core . . . I was due to start working for a law firm. Passed all the interviews and had been notified to report for work the following Monday . . . On Sunday, my sister and I were walking in the park when a blond boy who had a crush on me but was too bashful to speak, demonstrated his affection by throwing an apple core which struck me here. (*She indicates the area beneath her left eye*) When I woke up Monday morning, I had the most beautiful black eye you ever saw. Too embarrassed to start a new job looking like that, I called in sick. They called back to say the position had been filled by someone else . . . The next job I found was the one that brought your father and I together . . . I often think of that apple core and wonder what my life would be like if it had never been thrown.

TIMMY Everyone wonders about things like that.

NETTIE I was going in early to type up some dictation I'd taken the night before . . . Front Street was deserted . . . As I walked, I had the sensation of being watched . . . I glanced up at the office I was passing and saw this young man, your father, staring down . . . He regarded me intensely, almost angrily, for a moment,

199

then suddenly realized I was looking back at him and turned away . . . In that moment, I knew that that young man and I were not suited to each other . . . And at the same time I knew we would become involved . . . that it was inevitable.

TIMMY Why? You had others to choose from.

NETTIE Oh yes . . . All gentle, considerate men. All very much like my father . . . One of them was the baker from Paterson, New Jersey, that we always joke about.

TIMMY The fellow who brought a hatbox full of pastries whenever he called on you.

NETTIE Yes . . . What a sweet man . . . How he begged me to marry.

TIMMY What was it that drew you to Pop?

NETTIE I think it was his energy . . . a certain wildness. He was not like my father at all . . . I was attracted . . . and I was afraid. I've always been a little afraid of him . . . And then he was clearly a young man who was going places. Twenty-four when I met him and making well over a hundred a week. Great money in those days and his prospects were unlimited . . . Money was never plentiful in our house. We weren't poor like his people, you understand. Never without rent, or food, or tickets to the opera, or nice clothes. But still we weren't well-to-do . . . My father brought home stories from the hotel about the various bigwigs who came in and what they wore and how they talked and acted. And we went to the opera. And we had friends who were cultured. Musical Sunday afternoons. Those were Papa's happiest moments . . . Yes, I liked good things. Things that the baker from Paterson and the others could never give me . . . But your father surely would. The way he was going he would be a millionaire . . . That was his dream, you know—to be a millionaire by the time he was forty . . . Nineteen twenty-nine took care of that. He was never quite the same afterwards . . . But when I met him he was cock of the walk. Good-looking, witty young Irishman. Everyone liked him and those who didn't at least feared him because he was a fierce fellow. Everyone wanted to go into business with him. Everyone wanted to be social with him . . . He was immediately at home on a ship, a train . . . in any bar. Strangers thought he was magnificent. And he *was* . . . as long as the situation was impersonal . . . At his best in an impersonal situation . . . But that doesn't include the home, the family . . . The baker from Paterson was all tongue-tied outside, but in the home he would have been beautiful . . . Go to bed now.

(*He kisses her on the forehead*)

TIMMY Want the light off?

NETTIE Please.
(*He moves to the lamp, is about to turn it off, hesitates*)

TIMMY When I left this house three years ago, I blamed *him* for everything that was wrong here . . . When I came home, I blamed *you* . . . Now I suspect that no one's to blame . . . Not even me. (*He turns the light off*) Good night.

NETTIE Good night.
(TIMMY *exits into his room, closes the door. For a moment there is silence. Then . . .*)

NETTIE "Who loves you, Nettie?" . . . "You do, Papa." . . . "Why, Nettie?" . . . "Because I'm a nice girl, Papa."
Curtain

Scene 4

Time: Nine A.M. *Monday.*

At rise: JOHN *and* NETTIE *are in the kitchen.*

JOHN One word from you . . . That's all it would take.

NETTIE I'm not so sure.

JOHN Try.

NETTIE No.

JOHN Do you want him to go?

NETTIE No.

JOHN Then say something before it's too late.

NETTIE What do you want for breakfast?

JOHN Who cares about breakfast?

NETTIE Timmy's having scrambled eggs.

JOHN *Am I the only one who's upset by what's going on here?*

NETTIE No.

JOHN Then how can you just stand there?

NETTIE Would you feel better if I wept?

JOHN You'll weep when he's gone.

NETTIE But not now.

JOHN All I want you to do is tell him how you feel.

NETTIE He knows that.

JOHN You won't speak to him.

NETTIE   I can't.

JOHN   You're the one who'll miss him most . . . With me it's different. I've got my business.

NETTIE   I envy you.

JOHN   Just ask him to wait a couple of days and think it over.

NETTIE   After a couple of days, we'd be used to having him around. It would be that much harder to see him leave.

JOHN   He might change his mind. Might not want to leave.

NETTIE   He has to leave sometime.

JOHN   But not now. Not like this.

NETTIE   Twenty-second Street isn't the end of the world.

JOHN   If he leaves this house today I don't want to see him ever again!

NETTIE   If you say that to him, make it clear that you're speaking for yourself.

JOHN   Who's this fellow he's moving in with?

NETTIE   A boy he knew at high school.

JOHN   Everything he wants right here—food, clothing, a room of his own. And he has to move into a dirty cold-water flat.

NETTIE   I think I understand his feeling.

JOHN   Home two days and gone again. The neighbors will have a field day.

NETTIE   I'm going in to call him now.

JOHN   I want to see him alone.

NETTIE   If you're wise you won't start a row.

JOHN   *I want to see him alone.*

NETTIE   All right.
   (*She goes inside, knocks at* TIMMY's *door*)

TIMMY's VOICE   Come in.
   (*She enters the room, closes the door after her*)

JOHN (*Addresses* TIMMY's *place at the table*)   I understand you've decided to leave us . . . (*Not satisfied with
this opening, he tries another*) What's this nonsense
about your leaving? . . . (*And another*) Your mother
tells me you're moving out. I would like to know why.
(*The first part of this opening pleases him, the last part
doesn't. He tries variations on it:*) I *demand* to know
why . . . Would you be so good as to tell me why? . . .
Why, God-damn it?
   (*He is puzzling over these various approaches when*
   TIMMY *enters the kitchen*)

TIMMY   Good morning.

JOHN   Morning.

TIMMY   Mother said you wanted to see me.

JOHN   Sleep well?

TIMMY   Yes.

JOHN   Good . . .

TIMMY   You wanted to see me?

JOHN   Mother says you're leaving.

TIMMY   Yes.

JOHN   Rather sudden, isn't it?

TIMMY Not really.

JOHN Mind telling me why?

TIMMY I just think it's best.

JOHN For who?

TIMMY Everyone.

JOHN Crap! (TIMMY *starts from the room*) Wait. (*The note of entreaty in his voice causes* TIMMY *to halt*) I didn't mean that . . . The fact is I don't blame you for wanting to leave. I had no business hitting you.

TIMMY That's not why I'm going.

JOHN If there was any way I could undo last night, I would.

TIMMY It's not a question of last night.

JOHN If I had to do it over again I'd cut my arm off.

TIMMY Pop, listen—

JOHN I don't know what gets into me sometimes.

TIMMY Pop! (JOHN *looks at him*) I'm not leaving because of anything that happened last night . . . I always intended to leave.

JOHN You never mentioned it.

TIMMY I planned to stay a couple of weeks and then go.

JOHN A couple of days isn't a couple of weeks.

TIMMY It's not like I'm going to China.

JOHN Why two days instead of two weeks?

TIMMY Because I know that if I stay two weeks I'll *never* leave.

JOHN   If it's what I said yesterday, about me being the boss and you'd have to do what I said—forget it.

TIMMY   It's not that.

JOHN   I was just letting off steam.

TIMMY   *It's not that.*

JOHN   As far as I'm concerned you're a man—you can come and go as you please, do as you please. That goes for religion, drinking, anything.

TIMMY   How can I make you understand?

JOHN   Even girls. I know how it is to be your age. Give me a little advance notice and I'll see that you have the house to yourself whenever you want.

TIMMY   Pop, for Chrisake.

JOHN   (*Flares momentarily*) *What kind of language is that?* (*Then hastily*) I'm sorry. I didn't mean that. Talk any way you want.

TIMMY   I don't know what to say to you.

JOHN   What I said yesterday about the Jews, I was just trying to get a rise out of you.

TIMMY   I know.

JOHN   The time those bums from St. Matthew's jumped the I-cash-clothes man. I was the one who saved him.

TIMMY   I know.

JOHN   Whole crowd of people watching but I was the only one who did anything.

TIMMY   Do you think I could forget that?

JOHN   Stay another week. Just a week.

TIMMY   I can't.

JOHN   Stay till Wednesday.

TIMMY   No.

JOHN   Do you have any idea how your mother looked forward to your coming home?

TIMMY   Yes.

JOHN   Then how can you do it?

TIMMY   We're just going around in circles.

JOHN   What happens to the lake house?

TIMMY   What do you mean?

JOHN   Without you, what's the good of it?

TIMMY   I'll be spending time there.

JOHN   I thought we'd have a real summer together like before the war.

TIMMY   You're making this a lot tougher than it has to be.

JOHN   *Did you expect me to say nothing? Like her?* . . .

TIMMY   Are you through?

JOHN   (*Trying a new tack*)   I know what the trouble is. You know what the trouble is? You're like me . . . Stubborn . . . All the Clearys are stubborn . . . Would rather die than admit a mistake . . . Is that a fact? Yes or no?

TIMMY   I don't know.

JOHN   (*Points to himself*)   Well, here's one donkey who's seen the light. I've been wrong in my dealings with you and I admit it.

TIMMY Pop—

JOHN Not just wrong last night, but all along. Well, those days are gone forever, and I'll prove it . . . You know how much money I have?

TIMMY I don't want to know.

JOHN Fourteen thousand three hundred and fifty-seven dollars.

TIMMY Pop!

JOHN Plus a bit more in stocks . . . Now *you* admit that *you* made a mistake—admit you don't really want to leave and we'll forget the whole thing.

TIMMY I *don't* want to leave.

JOHN See—

TIMMY But I'm leaving.

JOHN (*Turning away*) *Then go and good riddance!*

TIMMY Listen to me.

JOHN The sooner the better.

TIMMY *Listen to me!* (*Pauses—then goes on quietly, intensely*) There was a dream I used to have about you and I . . . It was always the same . . . I'd be told that you were dead and I'd run crying into the street . . . Someone would stop me and ask why I was crying and I'd say, "My father's dead and he never said he loved me."

JOHN (*Trying unsuccessfully to shut out* TIMMY's *words*) I only tried to make you stay for her sake.

TIMMY I had that dream again last night . . . Was thinking about it this morning when something occurred to me that I'd never thought of before.

JOHN   She's the one who'll miss you.

TIMMY   It's true you've never said you love me. But it's also true that I've never said those words to you.

JOHN   I don't know what you're talking about.

TIMMY   I say them now—

JOHN   *I don't know what you're talking about.*

TIMMY   I love you, Pop. (*JOHN's eyes squeeze shut, his entire body stiffens, as he fights to repress what he feels) I love you. (For another moment, JOHN continues his losing battle, then, overwhelmed, turns, extends his arms. TIMMY goes to him. Both in tears, they embrace. NETTIE emerges from TIMMY's room, closes the door with emphasis to alert them to her approach. TIMMY and JOHN separate hastily*)

JOHN   What I said about the money—that's strictly between us.

TIMMY   I understand.
     (*NETTIE enters the kitchen. If she is aware of anything unusual in their appearance or manner, she doesn't show it*)

NETTIE   Ready for breakfast? (*They nod*) Sit down. (*They sit. She pours the coffee*)

NETTIE (*To TIMMY*)   Your bag is packed and ready to go.

TIMMY   I've changed my mind.

NETTIE   What?

TIMMY   I've changed my mind. I'm going to stay a few more days.

JOHN   I'm afraid that's out of the question. (*TIMMY and*

NETTIE *regard him incredulously*) When you said you were going, I called the painters. They're coming in to do your room tomorrow . . . You know how hard it is to get the painters. If we don't take them now, it'll be months before they're free again.

TIMMY Then I guess I better leave as scheduled.

JOHN I think so. (*To* NETTIE) Don't you?

NETTIE . . . Yes.
      (JOHN *tastes the coffee—scowls*)

JOHN I don't know why I bother to bring good coffee into this house. If it isn't too weak, it's too strong. If it isn't too strong, it's too hot. If it isn't . . .
                              Curtain

About the Author

FRANK D. GILROY made an auspicious theatre debut when his play *Who'll Save the Plowboy?* was presented at the Phoenix Theatre in 1962. Winner of an "Obie" as the Best American Play of the Year, *Who'll Save the Plowboy?* was published by Random House and has enjoyed numerous productions both here and abroad. *The Subject Was Roses* marks Mr. Gilroy's debut as a Broadway playwright. A product of television's Golden Age, he has written for such shows as Playhouse 90, Studio One, U.S. Steel, Omnibus and Kraft Theatre. Mr. Gilroy was born and educated in the Bronx. He graduated from DeWitt Clinton High School and entered the Army at eighteen. He served for two and a half years with the 89th Infantry Division—including eighteen months in the European Theatre. Mr. Gilroy attended Dartmouth College. A grant from Dartmouth enabled him to attend the Yale Drama School for one year. Thirty-nine years old, the playwright lives in upstate New York with his wife and three sons.